HOW TO START A COFFEE TRUCK

A Comprehensive Guide to Launching and Operating a Lucrative Mobile Coffee Business: From Concept to Profit-Generating Reality

Daryl V. Hatcher

COPYRIGHT NOTICE

COPYRIGHT © 2024 Daryl V. Hatcher

All rights reserved. The use of any part of this book, reproduced, transmitted in any form or by any means electronic, mechanical, photocopying, recording or otherwise, or stored in a retrieval system without the prior written consent of the publisher—or in the case of photocopying or other reprographic copying, license from the Copyright Licensing agency—is an infringement of the copyright law.

TABLE OF CONTENTS

INTRODUCTION 10
    Coffee Truck 11
    Why This Book? 11

CHAPTER 1   **THE COFFEE TRUCK DREAM** 12
    WHY A COFFEE TRUCK? 12
        Lower Costs 12
        Brand Recognition 13
        Flexibility and Mobility 13
        Community Engagement 13
    PITFALLS OF COFFEE TRUCK OWNERSHIP 14
        Lack of Planning 14
        Doing Everything Yourself 15
        Poor Service 15
        Ignoring Budgeting 15
        Poor Marketing 16
    ALTERNATIVE MOBILE COFFEE OPTIONS 16
        Coffee Carts 17
        Concession Stands 17
        Kiosks and Booths 18
        Gourmet Coffee Trucks 18

CHAPTER 2   **LAYING THE GROUNDWORK** 20
    WHY YOU NEED A PLAN 20
        Setting Goals 20
        Documentation 20
        Strategy Development 21
        Testing and Validation 21
    CREATING A BUSINESS PLAN 21
        Executive Summary 21
        Company Description 22
        Market Analysis 22
        Concept Development 22
        Business Operations 23

  Menu and Costs 23
  Target Market 23
  Location Strategy 24
  Branding, Marketing, and PR 24
  Company and Management Structure 25
  Financial Plan 25
 NICHE RESEARCH 25
  Identifying Your Niche 25
  Questions to Ask 26
  Naming Your Business 26

CHAPTER 3   **MANAGING YOUR MONEY** 28
 STARTUP COSTS 28
  Vehicle Cost 28
  Coffee Equipment 28
  Licenses and Permits 29
  Startup Inventory 29
  Operational Costs 29
  Labor Costs 30
  Marketing Expenses 30
 RAISING CAPITAL 30
  Debt Capital Sources 30
  Equity Capital Sources 31
  Crowdfunding 31
  Grants and Loans 31
 FINANCIAL MANAGEMENT 32
  Cost Management 32
  Profit Estimation 32
  Cash Flow Management 32
 COMMON FINANCIAL MISTAKES 33
  Ignoring Your Budget 33
  Underestimating Costs 33
  Overestimating Profits 33
  Neglecting Marketing 34
  Overpaying Yourself 34
  Not Saving for Taxes 34
  Skimping on Insurance 34
  Not Keeping Good Records 35
  Mixing Personal and Business Finances 35

                Not Planning for Growth 35
                Ignoring Financial Statements 35

CHAPTER 4 FINDING AND CUSTOMIZING YOUR TRUCK 38
          BUYING A TRUCK 38
               Cost Reduction Strategies 38
               Choosing the Right Truck. 39
               Finding Reliable Dealers 39
          CUSTOMIZING YOUR TRUCK 40
               Essential Equipment. 40
               Water and Power Systems 40
               Exterior Design. 41
               Final Design Approval 41

CHAPTER 5 NAVIGATING LEGAL REQUIREMENTS 44
          LEGAL CHALLENGES 44
               Understanding Local Laws. 44
               Preparing for Restrictive Regulations 45
          ORGANIZING YOUR LEGAL INFORMATION 46
               Sources of Information 46
               Organizational Tips 47
          REQUIRED PERMITS AND LICENSES 48
               Tax Registration and Business License 48
               Local Permits 49
               DBA Registration 50
               Employer Requirements 50
               Required Posters 51
               Miscellaneous Permits. 51
          INSURANCE NEEDS 52
               Questions to Ask 52
               Typical Coverage 53
               Additional Insured Certificates 54

CHAPTER 6 MARKETING STRATEGIES FOR SUCCESS 56
          PREPARATORY WORK. 56
               Competitor Analysis 56
               SWOT Analysis 57
               Creating a Marketing Overview 57
          DEVELOPING YOUR MARKETING PLAN. 58

PR and Media Mentions. 58
Event Participation 58
Branding. 59
Mobile Apps 59
Website Development 60
Social Media Strategy 60
Email Newsletters. 61
Contests and Promotions 61
Online Reviews 61
Marketing Tips 62
ENHANCING YOUR MARKETING EFFORTS 62
Making Marketing Fun 62
Health-Conscious Marketing 63
Customization 63
Behind-the-Scenes Content. 63
Customer Engagement. 64
Seasonal Promotions 64
Partnerships. 64
Event Calendars 65
Delivery Services 65
Text Marketing. 65
Press Releases 65

CHAPTER 7   CHOOSING THE BEST LOCATIONS 68
PRIME LOCATIONS. 68
Coffee Truck Parks. 68
Farmers Markets. 69
Business Districts 69
Gas Stations. 70
Bars and Nightlife Areas. 70
Festivals and Events 70
College Campuses 71
EVALUATING LOCATIONS 71
Location Assessment 71
Popular Events 72
FESTIVAL APPLICATIONS 73
Application Process 73
Tips for Success 74

CHAPTER 8 CRAFTING THE PERFECT MENU 76
MENU BASICS 76
Theme and Space Considerations 76
Pricing Strategies 77
MENU DESIGN 78
Highlighting Star Items 78
Visual Appeal 78
Proofreading 79
Concise Descriptions 79
Font and Color Choices 80
Feedback and Testing 81
Using Numbers 81
Clear labeling 82
MENU ENHANCEMENT TRICKS 82
Avoiding Dollar Signs 82
Pricing Strategies 83
Layout Tips 83
Highlighting Premium Items 84
Using Photos Effectively 84
Consistent Branding 85
Engaging Descriptions 86

CHAPTER 9 ENSURING COFFEE QUALITY AND SAFETY 88
COFFEE QUALITY CONTROL 88
Sourcing Quality Beans 88
Roasting Techniques 89
Brewing Methods 89
Consistency in Taste 90
SAFETY PRACTICES 91
Passing Inspections 91
Staff Training 91
Proper Washing and Cleaning 91
Produce Handling 92
Storage Protocols 92
Sanitization 92
Supply Inspection 93
INSPECTION PREPARATION 93
Handwashing Stations 93
Approved Sources 93

Temperature Control................................93
Cross Contamination Prevention..............94
Labeling Requirements............................94
Permit Display..94
Equipment Maintenance..........................94
Cleanliness Standards..............................94
Knowledge and Training..........................95

CHAPTER 10 GROWING AND SUSTAINING YOUR BUSINESS......96
HIRING AND TRAINING STAFF..................96
Recruitment Strategies...........................96
Training Programs..................................97
Creating an Employee Manual................98
LONG-TERM SUCCESS STRATEGIES..........98
Adaptability..98
Capital Reserves.....................................99
Grand Opening Tips................................99
Leadership by Example.........................100
Local Sourcing and Service Excellence..........100
Employee Satisfaction and Trust Building.......100
Consistency..101
Effective Communication.....................101
Cost Monitoring...................................102
BUSINESS EXPANSION............................102
Scaling Your Operations.......................102
Franchising Opportunities....................103
Diversifying Your Menu........................103
Exploring New Markets........................104

CONCLUSION...105
Final Thoughts......................................105
Encouragement and Motivation...........106

INTRODUCTION

Have you ever smelled fresh coffee and felt your mood lift? That's the magic a coffee truck can bring to any street corner. These rolling cafes are popping up everywhere, from busy city blocks to quiet suburban neighborhoods. They're not just selling coffee; they're selling an experience.

You might have seen these trucks and thought, "I could do that." Maybe you love making coffee and dream of running your own business. If so, you're in the right place. This book will show you how to turn that dream into reality.

Starting a coffee truck isn't as hard as opening a regular cafe, but it's not a walk in the park either. You need to know more than just how to make great coffee. You need to understand business basics, how to deal with rules and permits, and how to make your truck stand out from the crowd.

Don't worry if that sounds like a lot. We'll break it all down step by step. By the time you finish this book, you'll have a clear roadmap to start your own coffee truck business.

Coffee Truck

Think of a coffee truck as a cafe on wheels. It's a vehicle fitted with everything needed to make and serve coffee drinks. Some also offer snacks or light meals. The best part? You can drive your business to where the customers are.

Coffee trucks have some big advantages over regular cafes. They cost less to start and run. You're not stuck in one spot, so you can go where business is best. And let's face it, there's something exciting about buying coffee from a truck that draws people in.

But running a coffee truck isn't always easy. You have to be ready for anything. Bad weather can keep customers away. Your truck might break down. You need to be good at solving problems on the fly.

Why This Book?

I've been in the coffee truck business for five years now. When I started, I knew I loved coffee and wanted to run my own business. But I didn't know much else. I made a lot of mistakes and learned a lot of lessons the hard way.

Now, I want to share what I've learned with you. This book is like a cheat sheet for starting a coffee truck business. It's full of tips and tricks I wish someone had told me when I was starting out.

We'll talk about everything from choosing your truck to creating your menu. You'll learn how to handle money, deal with health inspectors, and keep customers coming back. I'll even share some of my biggest mistakes so you can avoid them.

But this book isn't just about facts and figures. It's about helping you believe in yourself and your dream. Starting a business is hard work, but it's also incredibly rewarding. My goal is to give you the knowledge and confidence to take that first step.

So, are you ready to join the coffee truck community? Are you excited to serve your own special blends to happy customers? If you're nodding your head, then let's get started. Your coffee truck adventure begins now!

CHAPTER 1
THE COFFEE TRUCK DREAM

A coffee truck business can be an amazing adventure where you get to share your love of coffee and make people's days a little brighter. But beyond the joy of serving up delicious brews, there are some very practical reasons why a coffee truck might be the perfect choice for you.

WHY A COFFEE TRUCK?

Lower Costs

Starting a coffee truck business is a chance to enter the world of entrepreneurship without breaking the bank. Unlike traditional brick-and-mortar cafes, coffee trucks don't require you to spend big money on rent, extensive renovations, or a large staff. You're essentially condensing all the magic of a cafe into a compact, mobile package.

Your kitchen, counter, storage, and even marketing billboard are all rolled into one vehicle. It's like the Swiss Army knife of the coffee world! This lean approach means you can start brewing profits faster than you can say "venti triple shot caramel macchiato."

But don't be fooled – while the initial investment is lower, you'll still need to budget for your truck, equipment, permits, and of course, top-notch coffee beans. Remember, we're aiming for a coffee truck, not a truck that happens to serve coffee!

Brand Recognition

Your coffee truck isn't just a vehicle; it's a moving billboard, a conversation starter, and a potential Instagram star all rolled into one! With the right design, your truck can become as recognizable as that famous mermaid logo (you know the one).

Think bold colors, eye-catching graphics, and a name that's punnier than a barista's t-shirt collection. "Bean There, Done That," "Espresso Yourself," or "The Daily Grind" – the possibilities are as endless as the ways to customize a latte!

But brand recognition goes beyond just looks. It's about creating an experience that people will remember and want to share. Maybe your thing is serving coffee with a side of dad jokes, or perhaps you've perfected the art of latte foam portraits. Whatever your unique selling point is, make sure it's as strong and distinctive as your signature brew.

Flexibility and Mobility

One of the sweetest perks of owning a coffee truck is the freedom to roam. Slow day at your usual spot? No problem! Just fire up the engine and cruise to where the customers are. You're not tied down to a single location, which means you can follow the ebb and flow of city life like a caffeinated nomad.

Morning rush hour? Park near office buildings and serve liquid productivity to bleary-eyed workers. Sunny afternoon? Head to the park and offer iced coffees to sunbathers. Big event in town? Be there, ready to caffeinate the masses. Your coffee truck is like a choose-your-own-adventure book, but with more espresso and less chance of being eaten by a grue.

This flexibility also extends to your work-life balance. While running a coffee truck isn't exactly a 9-to-5 job, it does give you more control over your schedule. Want to take a day off? You don't have to worry about keeping a storefront open. Need a vacation? Park that truck and hit the beach (just don't forget to secure any perishables first).

Community Engagement

Here's where owning a coffee truck gets really heartwarming – and I'm not just talking about the coffee. As a mobile business, you have the unique opportunity to become a beloved part of multiple communities. You're not just another faceless chain; you're the friendly neighborhood coffee wizard, bringing joy and java in equal measure.

You'll start to recognize your regular customers, learn their orders by heart, and become a part of their daily routines. There's something special about being the person who helps kickstart someone's day with a perfect cup of coffee and a friendly smile.

But it goes beyond just serving great coffee. Your truck can become a gathering spot, a place where people come not just for caffeine, but for conversation and connection. You might find yourself hosting impromptu community events, supporting local causes, or simply providing a listening ear to someone who needs it.

And let's not forget about the other local businesses and event organizers. As a mobile business, you have the opportunity to collaborate with a wide range of partners. From catering corporate events to partnering with local bakeries for your pastry selection, the possibilities for community involvement are as varied as the flavors in your syrup rack.

PITFALLS OF COFFEE TRUCK OWNERSHIP

Now, before you start revving your engine and grinding those beans, let's talk about some of the potential speed bumps on the road to coffee truck success. Don't worry – these aren't meant to deflate your tires, just to help you navigate the journey more smoothly.

Lack of Planning

You wouldn't start brewing a pour-over without first heating the water, right? The same goes for starting a coffee truck business. Diving in without a solid plan is like trying to make espresso without a machine – it's going to be a mess, and nobody's going to enjoy the results.

Your business plan is your roadmap. It should cover everything from your target market and pricing strategy to your equipment needs and marketing plans. Where will you source your beans? How will you handle waste disposal? What's your plan for bad weather days? These are all questions you need to answer before you even think about serving your first customer.

Don't forget about the legal side of things either. Permits, licenses, health inspections – they're about as fun as finding grounds in your coffee, but they're absolutely essential. Each city and state has different requirements for mobile food businesses, so do your homework. It might be tedious, but it's a lot better than getting shut down because you forgot to dot an 'i' or cross a 't'.

Doing Everything Yourself

I get it – your coffee truck is your baby, and nobody knows how to care for it better than you do. But trying to do everything yourself is a surefire recipe for burnout faster than you can say "red eye."

Yes, in the beginning, you might need to wear many hats – barista, mechanic, accountant, social media manager. But as your business grows, learn to delegate. Hire staff you trust, outsource tasks that aren't your strong suit, and give yourself time to focus on the big picture.

Remember, even the most sophisticated espresso machine needs regular maintenance to keep running smoothly. The same goes for you. Taking time for yourself isn't selfish – it's necessary for the long-term success of your business.

Poor Service

In the coffee truck business, service is just as important as the quality of your brew. You could be serving the most exquisite single-origin, shade-grown, hand-picked beans, but if your service leaves a bitter taste in people's mouths, they won't be coming back for a second cup.

Good service goes beyond just being polite (though that's certainly important). It's about efficiency, consistency, and creating a positive experience. Can you remember regular customers' orders? Can you keep a smile on your face even when you're dealing with the morning rush and someone's complaining that their triple, venti, half sweet, non-fat, caramel macchiato isn't exactly 120 degrees?

Train your staff well, lead by example, and always be open to feedback. Sometimes, turning a negative experience into a positive one can create a more loyal customer than if everything had gone perfectly in the first place.

Ignoring Budgeting

Money matters might not be as exciting as perfecting your latte art, but ignoring your finances is about as wise as using salt instead of sugar in your cookies. Proper budgeting is the difference between a thriving business and one that's always one broken grinder away from disaster.

Let's break down some numbers:

◊ - Initial investment: A food truck can cost anywhere from $50,000 to $200,000, depending on whether you buy new or used, and how you outfit it.

- ◊ - Equipment: Expect to spend $10,000 to $30,000 on coffee-making equipment alone.
- ◊ - Permits and licenses: These can range from $100 to $500 per year, depending on your location.
- ◊ - Inventory: Plan for about $1,000 to $2,000 per month for coffee beans, milk, syrups, and other supplies.
- ◊ - Fuel and maintenance: Budget around $500 to $1,000 per month for your truck.

Keep meticulous track of your income and expenses. Know your profit margins on each item. For example, a $3 latte might cost you $1 in ingredients, giving you a 66% profit margin. Understand your cash flow – because in a mobile business, it can be as unpredictable as the weather. Set aside at least 10% of your monthly revenue for repairs and upgrades – both for your truck and your equipment.

And please, for the love of coffee, don't fall into the trap of thinking all the money in the till is profit. That's a one-way ticket to financial espresso-induced panic attacks.

Poor Marketing

You might think that a bright, colorful truck parked on a busy street corner is all the marketing you need. And while it's true that your truck itself is a great marketing tool, relying on that alone is like trying to open a cafe and not telling anyone where it is.

In today's digital age, your online presence is just as important as your physical one. Social media isn't just for posting pretty latte art pictures (though those certainly help). Use it to announce your location, share your menu, and engage with your customers. Consider loyalty programs, partnerships with local businesses, and participation in community events.

But don't neglect good old-fashioned word-of-mouth either. Encourage reviews, offer referral discounts, and always, always provide an experience worth talking about. Your best marketing tool is a satisfied customer who can't wait to tell their friends about the amazing coffee truck they discovered.

ALTERNATIVE MOBILE COFFEE OPTIONS

While a full-fledged coffee truck offers numerous advantages, it's not the only way to enter the mobile coffee business. Depending on your budget, goals, and local regulations, you might find that one of these alternatives better suits your needs. Each option comes with its own set of pros and cons, and understanding these can help you make an informed decision about which path to take in your mobile coffee journey. Let's explore some alternatives that might be more your speed.

Coffee Carts

Think of coffee carts as the nimble little siblings of coffee trucks. They're smaller, simpler, and often a lot cheaper to start up. Perfect for those who want to dip their toes into the mobile coffee world without diving headfirst into the deep end.

Coffee carts are ideal for indoor locations like office buildings, hospitals, or universities. They're also great for events where space is at a premium. You might not be able to offer as extensive a menu as a full truck, but with the right equipment, you can still serve up a mean espresso or cold brew.

The best part? At the end of the day, you can pack everything up into a regular vehicle. No special driver's license required, and no worrying about where to park a big truck overnight.

However, keep in mind that with a smaller setup comes smaller capacity. You might need to restock more frequently, and you'll have less storage space for supplies. But hey, if you're just starting out or prefer a more intimate operation, a coffee cart could be your perfect match.

Concession Stands

Concession stands are the chameleons of the mobile food world. They can be as simple as a folding table with a coffee urn, or as elaborate as a mini cafe complete with seating area. The beauty of concession stands is their versatility – they can be set up pretty much anywhere there's foot traffic and a flat surface.

Festivals, farmers markets, sporting events – these are all prime territories for a coffee concession stand. You have more flexibility in terms of layout compared to a truck or cart, and you can adjust your setup based on the event or location.

The downside? You'll need to transport all your equipment to and from each location, which can be a workout in itself. And you're at the mercy of the weather unless you're in a covered area. But for those who love the idea of popping up in different locations and being part of various events, a concession stand could be just the ticket.

Kiosks and Booths

If you like the idea of a fixed location but aren't ready for a full-blown cafe, consider a coffee kiosk or booth. These are perfect for shopping malls, airport terminals, or busy downtown areas. You get the benefit of a regular customer base without the overhead of a traditional storefront.

Kiosks and booths offer more stability than a mobile operation – you don't have to worry about driving around or finding the perfect parking spot each day. They also allow for a bit more elaborate setup than a cart or concession stand. You might be able to offer a wider range of drinks and even some food items.

The trade-off is that you lose the flexibility of changing locations. You're also at the mercy of the foot traffic in your chosen spot. But if you can secure a prime location, a kiosk or booth can be a great way to build a loyal customer base and establish your brand.

Gourmet Coffee Trucks

Now we're talking! Gourmet coffee trucks are like the Rolls Royces of the mobile coffee world. These aren't your average joe trucks – they're decked out with top-of-the-line equipment, often custom-built to create a unique and memorable experience.

Gourmet coffee trucks can offer a full cafe menu, from espresso drinks to pour-overs, often with a selection of pastries or light bites. They might feature unique design elements like glass walls so customers can watch their drinks being made, or even seating areas for a more cafe-like experience.

The sky's the limit with gourmet trucks. Want to offer nitrogen-infused cold brew on tap? Go for it. Thinking about a truck that transforms into a pop-up seating area? Why not! These trucks are all about creating an experience that goes beyond just serving coffee.

Of course, all this comes with a higher price tag and more complex operations. But for those looking to make a big splash in the mobile coffee scene, a gourmet coffee truck could be the way to go.

So there you have it – a whirlwind tour of the mobile coffee landscape. Whether you're leaning towards a simple cart or dreaming of a state-of-the-art gourmet truck, remember that the most important ingredient in any coffee business is passion. Passion for great coffee, passion for excellent service, and passion for creating experiences that keep people coming back for refills.

CHAPTER 2
LAYING THE GROUNDWORK

You wouldn't build a house without a blueprint, would you? A business plan is your blueprint for success. It helps you define your goals, understand your market, and secure funding. It's essential for navigating the exciting, and sometimes challenging, world of coffee truck ownership.

WHY YOU NEED A PLAN
Setting Goals

Goals are the roadmap to your coffee truck dreams. Without them, you might end up driving in circles! Think about what you want to achieve. Do you want to serve 200 cups of coffee a day? Make $1500 in sales each week? Expand to a second truck in a year? Write these goals down. Make them specific and give them deadlines. This way, you'll know exactly what you're working towards.

Big goals can feel scary, so break them down into smaller steps. If you want to serve 200 cups a day, start with 50, then 100, and so on. Celebrate each milestone you reach. It'll keep you motivated and show you're on the right track.

Documentation

Keeping good records for your coffee truck business helps you see what's working and what's not. Write down everything - your coffee recipes, your daily sales, your expenses, even customer feedback. This information is gold! It'll help you make smart decisions as your business grows.

Think of documentation as telling your coffee truck's story. Years from now, you'll be able to look back and see how far you've come. Plus, if you ever need a loan or want to sell your business, good records will make everything much easier.

Strategy Development

A strategy turns your coffee truck dreams into reality. It's how you'll stand out in a sea of coffee options. Your strategy should cover everything from what kind of coffee you'll serve to how you'll find customers.

Think about what makes your coffee truck special. Maybe you use only fair-trade beans, or you have a unique brewing method. This is your "secret blend" - the thing that will make customers choose you over other coffee shops or trucks. Your strategy should focus on highlighting this unique aspect of your business.

Don't forget to plan for bumps in the road. What will you do if your espresso machine breaks down? How will you handle a sudden price increase in coffee beans? Having a plan B (and C and D) will help you stay calm when challenges come up.

Testing and Validation

Before you hit the road with your coffee truck, it's smart to test your ideas. Think of it as a dress rehearsal for your business. You could start by serving coffee to friends and family. Ask them for honest feedback about your drinks and pricing. Maybe set up a stand at a local fair or farmers market to see how strangers react to your offerings.

Pay attention to what people say and do. Do they finish their drinks? Do they come back for seconds? What questions do they ask? This information is super valuable. It can help you tweak your menu, adjust your prices, or even rethink your whole concept if needed.

Remember, it's much better to find out what works and what doesn't before you invest a lot of money in your coffee truck. Testing your ideas early can save you time, money, and heartache down the road.

CREATING A BUSINESS PLAN

Executive Summary

Think of the executive summary as the aroma of your coffee truck business - it should give people a quick, enticing preview of what you're offering. Even though it comes first in your business plan, it's often best to write it last. That way, you can include all the important details from the rest of your plan.

In your executive summary, talk about what makes your coffee truck special. Maybe you're bringing a new type of coffee drink to your area, or you have a unique way of serving your beverages. Mention your goals and how you plan to achieve them. Keep it short and snappy - aim for no more than a page. You want to grab people's attention and make them eager to read more.

Company Description

Here's where you get to brag a little about your coffee truck idea. Describe your business in detail. What kind of coffee will you serve? Why did you choose this type of coffee? What experience do you have that makes you the right person to run this coffee truck?

Don't forget to mention the legal stuff too. Will you be a sole proprietorship, a partnership, or an LLC? Each has its pros and cons, so do some research to figure out which is best for you. Also, talk about where your coffee truck will operate. Will you stick to one neighborhood or travel around the city?

Market Analysis

Time to put on your detective hat! Market analysis means figuring out who your customers will be and who your competition is. Start by looking at other coffee shops and trucks in your area. What do they serve? How much do they charge? What do customers say about them?

Next, think about your potential customers. Who are they? Where do they hang out? What kind of coffee do they like? The more you know about your market, the better you can tailor your coffee truck to meet their needs.

Don't forget to look at bigger trends too. Are there new office buildings or housing developments popping up? These could be great opportunities for your coffee truck.

Concept Development

This is where you get to let your creativity shine! Your concept is more than just the coffee you'll serve - it's the whole experience you want to create for your customers. Think about your truck's design, your menu layout, even the music you'll play.

Your concept should match your coffee. If you're serving artisanal pour-overs, maybe your truck looks like a cozy cafe on wheels. If you're doing quick espresso drinks, perhaps your truck is sleek and modern. The goal is to create a cohesive experience that customers will remember and want to come back to.

Business Operations

Now we're getting into the nitty-gritty of how your coffee truck will run day-to-day. Think about everything that needs to happen to get coffee from your truck to your customers. How will you order beans and supplies? Where will you store them? How will you prep your drinks?

Don't forget about the less exciting but super important stuff too. How will you handle money? What about cleaning and maintenance? Will you need employees, and if so, how will you train them?

It's also smart to think about how you'll handle busy times and slow times. Maybe you'll offer catering services or sell bagged coffee during slower periods. Planning for these details now will make your life much easier once you're up and running.

Menu and Costs

Your menu is the heart of your coffee truck. It should reflect your concept and appeal to your target market. Start by listing all the drinks you want to serve. Then, figure out how much each one costs to make. This includes not just the coffee, but also things like cups, lids, milk, syrups, and even the fuel for your truck.

Once you know your costs, you can set your prices. A good rule of thumb is to aim for beverage costs to be about 25-35% of your selling price. So if a latte costs you $1 to make, you might sell it for $3-$4. But remember, you need to consider what your competitors charge and what your customers are willing to pay too.

Don't make your menu too big. It's better to do a few drinks really well than to offer a huge menu that's just okay. And leave some room to add specials or seasonal drinks to keep things interesting.

Target Market

Who are your ideal customers? The more specific you can be, the better. Instead of saying "everyone who likes coffee," think "office workers in downtown who want a quick, quality coffee under $5." Understanding your target market helps you make smart decisions about everything from your menu to your marketing.

Think about where your target market hangs out, both in real life and online. Do they use Instagram a lot? Maybe that's where you should focus your social media efforts. Do they work in a particular area? That could be a great place to park your truck.

Remember, your target market might change depending on the time of day or the day of the week. Morning commuters and afternoon coffee breakers are often very different groups!

Location Strategy

For a coffee truck, location is everything. You need to be where your customers are, when they're craving caffeine. Start by making a list of potential spots. Think about foot traffic, parking, and local regulations. Some cities have specific areas where food and beverage trucks are allowed to operate.

Don't just stick to one spot. Try out different locations and keep track of how well you do in each. Over time, you'll figure out your best spots for different times of day or days of the week.

Also consider special events like festivals, farmers markets, or outdoor concerts. These can be great opportunities to reach a lot of customers in one day. Just make sure you have the right permits and can handle the volume.

Branding, Marketing, and PR

Your brand is more than just your logo - it's the whole personality of your coffee truck. It should come through in everything from your truck's design to how you talk to customers on social media. Think about what makes your coffee truck unique and how you can showcase that in your branding.

Marketing is how you get the word out about your awesome coffee truck. Social media is huge for coffee businesses - people love to share pictures of beautiful latte art! Consider starting an Instagram account or a Facebook page for your truck. Post mouth-watering photos of your drinks and let people know where you'll be each day.

Don't forget about old-school marketing too. Flyers in local businesses or a sign on your truck can be very effective. And always be on the lookout for opportunities to get some free publicity. Local food and drink bloggers or news stations are often interested in featuring new coffee businesses.

Company and Management Structure

Even if you're starting small, it's important to think about how your business will be structured. Will you be the only barista at first? Do you have a partner? How will you divide responsibilities?

As you grow, you might need to hire employees. Think about what roles you'll need to fill. Another barista? A cashier? Someone to handle social media? Write job descriptions for each role so you're clear on who will do what.

Don't forget about the boring but important stuff like payroll and taxes. You might want to consult with an accountant or lawyer to make sure you're setting everything up correctly from the start.

Financial Plan

This is where you crunch the numbers. Start by estimating your startup costs. This includes buying or leasing your truck, coffee equipment, initial inventory, permits, and insurance. Don't forget to include some extra money for unexpected expenses.

Next, project your income and expenses for at least the first year. Be realistic - it often takes time for a new business to become profitable. Include all your ongoing costs like coffee beans, milk, cups, fuel, maintenance, and labor.

Finally, think about how you'll fund your coffee truck. Will you use savings? Take out a loan? Look for investors? Each option has pros and cons, so consider them carefully.

Remember, your financial plan is a living document. You'll need to update it regularly as you learn more about your business and your market.

NICHE RESEARCH

Identifying Your Niche

Finding your niche is what makes you special and different from all the other coffee shops and trucks out there. Maybe you make the best cold brew in town, or you specialize in single-origin pour-overs. Whatever it is, your niche should be something you're passionate about and that fills a gap in the market.

To find your niche, start by thinking about what you love about coffee. Then, look at what's already out there. Is there something missing? Could you do something better or different? Don't be afraid to get creative. Some of the most successful coffee trucks have very unique concepts.

Remember, your niche isn't just about the coffee. It could also be about how you serve it, where you serve it, or who you serve it to. Maybe you're the only coffee truck that caters to night shift workers, or perhaps you use only organic, locally-roasted beans.

Questions to Ask

When you're figuring out your niche, ask yourself these questions:
- ◊ -What kind of coffee do I love to make and drink?
- ◊ -What's missing in my local coffee scene?
- ◊ -Who are my potential customers and what do they want in a coffee experience?
- ◊ -What unique skills or experiences do I have that I could bring to a coffee truck?
- ◊ -How can I stand out from other coffee shops and trucks?

Take your time answering these questions. Talk to friends, family, and potential customers. Do some taste tests. The more thought you put into this stage, the stronger your concept will be.

Naming Your Business

Choosing a name for your coffee truck is a big deal. It's often the first thing people will learn about your business, so it needs to make a good impression. Your name should reflect your niche and give people a hint about what kind of coffee experience you offer.

Brainstorm a bunch of ideas. Don't worry about being perfect at first - just get all your ideas down. Then start narrowing them down. A good coffee truck name should be:
- ◊ -Easy to say and spell
- ◊ -Memorable
- ◊ -Related to coffee or your concept
- ◊ -Not too similar to other coffee businesses in your area

Once you have a shortlist, ask for opinions from friends and family. You could even do a poll on social media to see which names people like best.

Before you make your final decision, do a quick online search to make sure no one else is using the name. You should also check if the website domain and social media handles are available for your chosen name.

Remember, your name will be with you for a long time, so choose something you really love. It should make you smile every time you see it on the side of your coffee truck!

CHAPTER 3
MANAGING YOUR MONEY

Money matters can be tricky, but they're crucial for your coffee truck's success. Think of your finances as the fuel that keeps your business running smoothly. Without proper financial management, even the best coffee and the coolest truck can't save your business. So, let's roll up our sleeves and dig into the dollars and cents of running a coffee truck!

STARTUP COSTS

Vehicle Cost

Your coffee truck is more than just a set of wheels - it's your mobile cafe. The cost can vary widely depending on whether you buy new, used, or decide to lease. A new, fully-equipped coffee truck might set you back $50,000 to $100,000. A used truck could cost anywhere from $20,000 to $40,000, but you might need to spend extra on renovations and equipment.

Don't forget about ongoing costs like insurance, registration, and maintenance. These can add up to several thousand dollars a year. If you're handy, you might save money by buying a regular truck and converting it yourself. Just make sure you follow all health and safety regulations.

Coffee Equipment

Great coffee needs great equipment. At a minimum, you'll need an espresso machine, grinder, refrigerator, and water filtration system. Depending on your menu, you might also want a blender, ice maker, or cold brew system.

A commercial-grade espresso machine can cost anywhere from $5,000 to $20,000. A good grinder might be another $1,000 to $2,000. Don't skimp on these - they're the heart of your business. Budget at least $10,000 to $30,000 for all your equipment.

Licenses and Permits

Before you serve your first cup, you'll need the right paperwork. The exact licenses and permits you need will depend on where you operate, but common ones include:

- ◊ - Business license
- ◊ - Food handler's permit
- ◊ - Health department permit
- ◊ - Mobile food vendor license
- ◊ - Parking permits

These can cost anywhere from a few hundred to a few thousand dollars. Some need to be renewed annually, so factor that into your budget. It's a good idea to check with your local government offices to make sure you have everything you need.

Startup Inventory

You can't make coffee without beans! Your initial inventory will include coffee beans, milk, syrups, cups, lids, stirrers, and napkins. Don't forget about cleaning supplies and any food items you plan to sell.

How much you spend will depend on your menu and expected sales volume. A good starting point might be $2,000 to $4,000. It's better to start with a smaller inventory and restock often than to overbuy and risk waste.

Operational Costs

These are the day-to-day expenses of running your coffee truck. They include:

- ◊ - Fuel for your truck
- ◊ - Propane for your equipment
- ◊ - Electricity (if you use a generator)
- ◊ - Water
- ◊ - Waste disposal

You might spend $500 to $1,000 a month on these costs. Keep track of these expenses carefully - they can eat into your profits if you're not watching.

Labor Costs

Even if you plan to be a one-person show at first, you should budget for labor costs. As your business grows, you might need to hire help. A part-time barista might cost $10 to $15 an hour, depending on your location and their experience.

Don't forget to factor in payroll taxes and any benefits you plan to offer. A good rule of thumb is to budget 1.25 to 1.4 times an employee's hourly wage to cover all labor-related costs.

Marketing Expenses

Getting the word out about your coffee truck is crucial. Your marketing budget might include:

- ◊ - Social media advertising
- ◊ - Printed flyers or menus
- ◊ - Business cards
- ◊ - Website hosting
- ◊ - Branded merchandise (like t-shirts or mugs)

You might spend $500 to $2,000 on initial marketing, with ongoing costs of $200 to $500 per month. As your business grows, you can adjust your marketing budget based on what works best for you.

RAISING CAPITAL

Now that you know how much you need, let's talk about where that money might come from.

Debt Capital Sources

Borrowing money is one way to fund your coffee truck. Options include:

Bank loans: Traditional banks offer business loans, but they often require good credit and collateral.

SBA loans: The Small Business Administration backs loans from regular banks, often with better terms for small businesses.

Credit cards: These can be useful for small purchases, but be careful of high interest rates.

Personal loans: You might be able to borrow against your home equity or retirement savings, but be cautious about risking your personal assets.

The upside of debt is that you keep full ownership of your business. The downside is that you have to pay the money back with interest, which can strain your cash flow in the early days.

Equity Capital Sources

With equity funding, you sell a part of your business in exchange for money. This might mean:

Angel investors: Wealthy individuals who invest in small businesses.

Venture capital: Firms that invest in high-growth potential businesses (though this is rare for coffee trucks).

Friends and family: People you know who believe in your vision and want to support you.

The advantage of equity funding is that you don't have to pay the money back. The downside is that you give up some control of your business.

Crowdfunding

Platforms like Kickstarter or GoFundMe let you raise money from lots of people in small amounts. This can be a great way to gauge interest in your coffee truck idea. You might offer rewards like free coffee or branded merchandise to encourage people to contribute.

Crowdfunding can be a lot of work, but it's also a way to build buzz about your business before you even open.

Grants and Loans

Look for special programs in your area that support small businesses. Some options might include:

- ◊ -Local economic development grants
- ◊ -Minority or women-owned business grants
- ◊ -Veteran-owned business loans
- ◊ -Food truck-specific loan programs

These can offer better terms than traditional loans, but they often have specific requirements and can be competitive.

FINANCIAL MANAGEMENT

Once you've got your startup money, you need to manage it wisely.

Budgeting

A budget is your financial roadmap. It helps you plan where your money will go and track where it actually went. Your budget should include all your expected income and expenses. Be as detailed as possible.

Review your budget regularly - at least monthly at first. This will help you spot trends and make adjustments quickly.

Cost Management

Keeping your costs under control is key to making a profit. Some tips:

◊ -Shop around for suppliers to get the best prices on coffee beans and other supplies.

◊ -Buy in bulk when it makes sense, but be careful not to overstock perishable items.

◊ -Track your inventory closely to reduce waste.

◊ -Look for ways to be more energy-efficient to cut fuel and electricity costs.

Profit Estimation

To estimate your profits, you need to know your costs and your prices. Let's say a latte costs you $1 to make (including the cup, milk, coffee, and a portion of your overhead costs) and you sell it for $4. Your profit on that latte is $3.

But don't count all that as money in your pocket! Some of it needs to go back into the business for things like equipment upgrades or marketing.

A good target is to aim for a 60-70% gross profit margin (that's your sales minus your direct costs, divided by your sales).

Cash Flow Management

Cash flow is the lifeblood of your business. It's about timing - making sure you have money when you need to pay your bills. Some tips for managing cash flow:

◊ -Try to negotiate good terms with your suppliers, like 30 days to pay.

◊ -Consider offering discounts for cash payments to get money in hand faster.

- -Keep some cash reserves for unexpected expenses or slow periods.
- -Use accounting software to track your cash flow and forecast future needs.

COMMON FINANCIAL MISTAKES

Even with careful planning, it's easy to make financial mistakes. Knowing the common pitfalls can help you avoid them.

Ignoring Your Budget

A budget only works if you use it. Some coffee truck owners make a budget, then forget about it. This is like having a map but never looking at it – you're likely to get lost.

Fix it: Review your budget regularly. At least once a month, compare your actual spending to your budget. If there are big differences, figure out why. Maybe you need to adjust your budget, or maybe you need to change your spending habits.

Underestimating Costs

It's easy to forget about small expenses or unexpected costs. These can add up quickly and eat into your profits.

Fix it: Keep detailed records of ALL your expenses, even small ones. Include things like:

- -Cleaning supplies
- -Vehicle maintenance
- -Parking fees
- -Credit card processing fees
- -Taxes

When planning, add a "miscellaneous" category to your budget for unexpected costs. A good rule of thumb is to add 10% to your estimated expenses to cover surprises.

Overestimating Profits

New business owners often think they'll be profitable faster than they actually are. This can lead to overspending or taking on too much debt.

Fix it: Be conservative in your profit estimates, especially for the first year. It's better to be pleasantly surprised by higher profits than stressed by lower ones. Also, remember that seasons can affect your business. You might be busy in summer but slower in winter. Plan for these fluctuations.

Neglecting Marketing

When money is tight, marketing is often the first thing cut. But without marketing, how will new customers find you?

Fix it: Include marketing in your regular budget. It doesn't have to be expensive. Social media, local partnerships, and community events can be low-cost ways to spread the word. Track which marketing efforts bring in customers so you know where to focus your money.

Overpaying Yourself

You started this business to make money, right? But paying yourself too much too soon can drain your business's resources.

Fix it: In the beginning, pay yourself enough to cover your basic needs, but reinvest most profits back into the business. As your coffee truck becomes more stable and profitable, you can increase your pay. Always separate your personal and business finances to keep things clear.

Not Saving for Taxes

Taxes can be a nasty surprise if you're not prepared. Some new business owners spend all their profit, then struggle to pay their tax bill.

Fix it: Set aside money for taxes with every sale. A good rule of thumb is to save 25-30% of your profit for taxes. Keep this money in a separate account so you're not tempted to spend it.

Skimping on Insurance

Proper insurance seems expensive until something goes wrong. Then it's a lifesaver.

Fix it: Get the right insurance coverage from the start. This usually includes:
- ◊ -General liability insurance
- ◊ -Vehicle insurance
- ◊ -Property insurance (for your equipment)

◊ -Workers' compensation (if you have employees)

Talk to an insurance agent who understands food truck businesses to make sure you're properly covered.

Not Keeping Good Records

Messy or incomplete financial records can cause big problems. You might miss bill payments, lose track of who owes you money, or get in trouble with taxes.

Fix it: Set up a good bookkeeping system from day one. This doesn't have to be complicated – a simple spreadsheet can work when you're starting out. As you grow, consider using accounting software or hiring a bookkeeper.

Keep all receipts and invoices. Take time each week to update your records. This makes tax time much easier and helps you spot financial trends in your business.

Mixing Personal and Business Finances

Using your personal credit card for business expenses or your business account for personal purchases can create a big mess.

Fix it: Open separate bank accounts and credit cards for your business. Use these only for business expenses. This makes it much easier to track your business finances and simplifies your taxes.

Not Planning for Growth

Success can bring its own problems. If your coffee truck takes off, you might struggle to keep up with demand.

Fix it: Have a plan for growth. This might include:

◊ -Saving money to buy better equipment
◊ -Training employees to take on more responsibility
◊ -Researching what you'd need to do to add a second truck

Think about what success looks like for you and plan accordingly.

Ignoring Financial Statements

Financial statements like profit and loss reports or balance sheets can seem boring or confusing. But they tell you important things about your business's health.

Fix it: Learn to read and understand basic financial statements. You don't need to be an accountant, but knowing what these numbers mean helps you make better business decisions. Consider taking a basic business finance class or working with a mentor who can explain these concepts.

Managing the financial side of your coffee truck business might seem overwhelming at first. But with careful planning, good habits, and a willingness to learn, you can build a strong financial foundation for your business.

CHAPTER 4
FINDING AND CUSTOMIZING YOUR TRUCK

Your coffee truck will be the heart of your business. It's where you'll create delicious drinks, interact with customers, and build your brand. Choosing the right truck and customizing it to fit your needs is crucial for your success. Let's explore how to find the perfect vehicle and turn it into your dream coffee truck.

BUYING A TRUCK
Cost Reduction Strategies

Buying a truck can be one of the biggest expenses when starting your coffee truck business. But there are ways to keep costs down without sacrificing quality.

First, consider buying a used truck. Many food truck owners upgrade their vehicles after a few years, so you can often find well-maintained used trucks at a fraction of the cost of a new one. Just make sure to have a mechanic check it out before you buy.

Another option is to lease a truck. This can lower your upfront costs and give you the flexibility to upgrade as your business grows. Some companies even offer lease-to-own options, which can be a good middle ground.

Don't forget to shop around. Get quotes from multiple dealers and be willing to negotiate. Sometimes, you can get a better deal if you're willing to pay cash or if you buy during the off-season (usually winter in colder climates).

If you're handy, you might consider buying a regular truck and converting it yourself. This can save money, but make sure you understand all the health and safety regulations before going this route.

Choosing the Right Truck

The right truck for your coffee business depends on several factors. First, think about size. A larger truck gives you more space to work and store supplies, but it also costs more to buy and operate. A smaller truck might be easier to maneuver and park, especially in busy urban areas.

Consider the layout of the truck. You'll need space for your coffee equipment, storage for supplies, and a service window. Some trucks have the service window on the side, while others have it at the back. Think about how you'll set up your workflow and choose a layout that makes sense for you.

Pay attention to the engine and mechanical condition of the truck. A newer truck might cost more upfront but could save you money on repairs down the road. If you're buying used, ask for maintenance records and have a trusted mechanic inspect it.

Think about fuel efficiency too. A more fuel-efficient truck will save you money in the long run, especially if you plan to drive to different locations frequently.

Finally, make sure the truck meets all local health and safety regulations for mobile food businesses. These can vary by location, so check with your local health department before making a purchase.

Finding Reliable Dealers

Finding a trustworthy dealer can make the process of buying a truck much smoother. Start by asking other food truck owners in your area for recommendations. They might know of reputable dealers or even be looking to sell their own trucks.

Look for dealers who specialize in food trucks or commercial vehicles. They'll understand your needs better than a general car dealership. Check online reviews and ratings for any dealer you're considering.

Don't be afraid to ask lots of questions. A good dealer should be able to explain the features of different trucks, discuss customization options, and provide information about warranties and after-sale support.

If possible, visit the dealer in person to see the trucks up close. This gives you a chance to check the condition of the vehicles and get a feel for how they might work for your business.

CUSTOMIZING YOUR TRUCK

Essential Equipment

Once you have your truck, it's time to outfit it with all the equipment you need to make great coffee. At a minimum, you'll need:

An espresso machine: This is the heart of your coffee setup. Choose a commercial-grade machine that can handle high volume.

A coffee grinder: Freshly ground coffee makes a big difference in quality. Look for a grinder that's fast and consistent.

A refrigerator: You'll need this for milk and other perishables. Make sure it's powerful enough to keep things cold even on hot days.

A sink: Health regulations usually require a hand-washing sink and a separate sink for washing equipment.

Storage: You'll need places to store cups, lids, stirrers, and other supplies.

A point-of-sale system: This could be as simple as a cash box or as complex as a tablet-based system that takes credit cards.

When choosing equipment, think about your menu and workflow. If you plan to offer blended drinks, you'll need a good blender. If pour-over coffee is your specialty, make sure you have space for that setup.

Don't forget about smaller items like thermometers, timers, and scales. These can make a big difference in the consistency of your drinks.

Water and Power Systems

A reliable water and power system is crucial for your coffee truck. You'll need a clean water tank large enough to last through a busy day, plus a separate tank for wastewater. Some trucks have built-in water heaters, while others use the espresso machine to heat water.

For power, you have a few options. Many coffee trucks use generators, which allow you to operate anywhere. However, generators can be noisy and require fuel. Another option is to use a battery system with an inverter, which is quieter but may not provide as much power.

Some trucks have hookups for "shore power," allowing you to plug into an electrical outlet when available. This can be useful for events or regular locations where power is provided.

Make sure your electrical system can handle all your equipment running at once. You don't want to blow a fuse in the middle of the morning rush!

Exterior Design

The outside of your truck is a giant advertisement for your business. A great design can attract customers and help build your brand.

Start by choosing colors that reflect your brand personality. Bright colors can make your truck stand out, while more muted tones might give a sophisticated feel.

Your logo should be prominently displayed and easy to read from a distance. Consider adding your menu to the side of the truck so customers can see what you offer.

Think about practical elements too. A large service window makes it easier to interact with customers. Awnings can provide shade for customers waiting in line.

Some coffee trucks add fun elements like chalkboards for daily specials or even small shelves where customers can rest their drinks while chatting.

Remember that your truck will be seen on the road too. Make sure your contact information and social media handles are visible so people can find you later.

Final Design Approval

Before you start serving coffee, you'll need to get your truck design approved by local authorities. This usually involves an inspection to make sure your truck meets health and safety standards.

The inspector will check things like:

- ◊ -The materials used in your truck (they should be easy to clean and food-safe)
- ◊ -Your water and waste systems
- ◊ -Your refrigeration and hot-holding equipment
- ◊ -Your fire suppression system (if you have cooking equipment)
- ◊ -Your electrical system

They'll also want to see that you have the right permits and licenses displayed.

It's a good idea to schedule a preliminary inspection before you finish your build-out. This way, you can catch any potential issues early and avoid costly changes later.

Once you pass inspection, you'll be ready to hit the road and start serving amazing coffee to your community!

CHAPTER 5
NAVIGATING LEGAL REQUIREMENTS

Starting a coffee truck business involves more than just brewing great coffee and serving it with a smile. You'll need to navigate a complex maze of legal requirements to keep your business running smoothly and avoid costly fines or shutdowns. Let's break down these challenges step by step so you can tackle them with confidence and set your coffee truck up for success.

LEGAL CHALLENGES
Understanding Local Laws

Every city and county has its own set of rules for food trucks, and coffee trucks often fall under these regulations. These laws can cover everything from where you can park your truck to how you handle food safety, and they can vary widely from one location to another.

Start your legal journey by contacting your local health department. They're the go-to source for information about food safety regulations and required permits. Ask them about food handler's certifications. You and your staff might need to complete a food safety course. This course will teach you about proper food handling, storage temperatures, and how to prevent contamination. It's not just about following rules - it's about keeping your customers safe and healthy.

Next, ask about equipment requirements. The health department might require specific types of sinks, refrigerators, or water heaters. For example, you might need a three-compartment sink for washing, rinsing, and sanitizing equipment. You'll also need to know about inspection schedules. Find out how often your truck will need to be inspected and what inspectors look for. They might check things like the cleanliness of your equipment, the temperature of your refrigerator, and how you store your ingredients.

After talking to the health department, check with your city's business development office. They can provide valuable information about zoning laws. Some areas might not allow food trucks at all, while others have designated food truck zones. You don't want to invest in a truck only to find out you can't operate in your chosen area.

Ask about parking restrictions too. You might be limited in how long you can stay in one spot or where you can park overnight. Some cities require food trucks to move every few hours, which can make it hard to build a regular customer base. Operating hours are another important factor. Some cities restrict when food trucks can operate, especially in residential areas. You might not be allowed to start serving early morning coffee if you're near homes.

Distance requirements are another thing to consider. You might need to stay a certain distance away from brick-and-mortar restaurants or other food trucks. This is often to protect existing businesses from competition.

Don't forget to investigate noise regulations. Your coffee grinder and espresso machine might be louder than you think, and some areas have strict rules about noise levels, especially early in the morning or late at night. You might need to invest in quieter equipment or sound-proofing measures.

Preparing for Restrictive Regulations

Some areas have very strict rules for food trucks. These might include limits on operating hours. You might be restricted to certain times of day or days of the week. This can be challenging if you want to serve morning commuters but aren't allowed to operate until later in the day.

Requirements to move your truck every few hours can also be tough. This can make it challenging to build a regular customer base. You might just be getting into a good flow of customers when you have to pack up and move.

Bans on operating near brick-and-mortar restaurants are common in some areas. This is often due to pressure from established businesses who worry about competition. It can severely limit where you can park your truck, especially in busy downtown areas.

Some cities have restrictions on where you can prepare food. They might require all food prep to be done in a licensed commercial kitchen, not in your truck. This means you'd need to rent kitchen space in addition to your truck, which adds to your costs.

A few cities have even started requiring mandatory GPS tracking for food trucks. They want to be able to monitor where trucks are operating at all times. This can feel invasive, but it's becoming more common in some areas.

If you find the regulations in your area are too restrictive, you have several options. You could look for a nearby city with more food truck-friendly laws. Sometimes crossing a city line can make a big difference in regulations. You might find that a neighboring town is much more welcoming to food trucks.

Another option is to focus on catering and special events rather than daily street vending. These often have different rules and can be more flexible. You might be able to operate at festivals, farmers markets, or private events even if street vending is restricted.

Getting involved with local food truck associations can also help. These groups often work to change unfair laws and create better conditions for mobile food businesses. They can also provide valuable advice and support. You might be able to join forces with other food truck owners to lobby for more favorable regulations.

If all else fails, you might need to consider a different business model. A coffee cart or kiosk might have different regulations than a full truck. Or you might look into a brick-and-mortar location instead. The important thing is to understand the rules before you invest too much money in your truck.

ORGANIZING YOUR LEGAL INFORMATION

Sources of Information

Gathering all the legal information you need can feel overwhelming. But don't worry - there are plenty of resources available to help you. Let's look at some good places to start your research.

Your first stop should be City Hall or your local government website. Look for sections on business licenses, health permits, and zoning laws. Many cities now have dedicated pages for food truck regulations. These pages often have downloadable forms, fee schedules, and contact information for relevant departments.

The Small Business Administration (SBA) is another great resource. They offer free resources and advice for new business owners. Check out their online learning center for courses on business law and regulations. They also have local offices where you can get personalized advice.

Local food truck associations can be incredibly helpful. These groups often have guides to local laws and can offer advice based on experience. They might also offer group rates on insurance or legal services. Plus, you'll get to connect with other food truck owners who can share their experiences.

Don't be afraid to reach out to other food truck owners directly. Most are happy to share what they've learned about navigating local regulations. You might even find a mentor who can guide you through the process.

If you're feeling overwhelmed, consider talking to a lawyer who specializes in small business or food service law. While this can be expensive, a consultation might save you headaches down the road. Some lawyers offer free initial consultations where you can get a sense of what legal issues you need to be aware of.

Your local SCORE chapter is another great resource. SCORE is a nonprofit organization that provides free business mentoring. They can often connect you with experts in local business law who can guide you through the regulatory maze.

Finally, consider attending food truck conferences and expos. These events often include seminars on legal issues facing food truck owners. You'll get to learn from experts and connect with other food truck owners from around the country.

Organizational Tips

Once you start gathering information, you'll need a system to keep it all organized. Good organization will save you time and stress in the long run. Here are some detailed tips to help you stay on top of your legal paperwork.

Start by creating a binder or digital folder for all your legal documents. Divide it into sections for different types of permits and regulations. You might have sections for health department rules, business licenses, parking regulations, and employee-related documents. Consider using color-coded tabs for easy reference. This way, you can quickly find what you need when an inspector asks to see a specific document.

Next, make a checklist of all the permits and licenses you need. Include due dates for renewals, costs, and where to obtain or renew each item. Update this list regularly as laws change. You might want to create a spreadsheet with columns for the permit name, issuing agency, cost, renewal date, and any special requirements.

Keeping a calendar of important dates is crucial. Mark inspection dates, permit renewals, and any deadlines for submitting paperwork. Set reminders on your phone or computer several weeks in advance so you don't miss any deadlines. Missing a renewal date could result in fines or even having to shut down your truck temporarily.

Save contact information for relevant government offices. Include names of specific people you've spoken with, as well as their direct phone numbers and email addresses when possible. Having a specific person to contact can make resolving issues much easier.

Consider using a cloud storage service to keep digital copies of all your documents. This way, you can access them from anywhere, even if you're not in your truck. Make sure to use strong passwords and two-factor authentication to protect sensitive information. You don't want anyone getting access to your business's private documents.

Create a "quick reference guide" with the most important information and keep a copy in your truck. This might include your license numbers, inspection dates, and emergency contact numbers. If an inspector shows up unexpectedly, you'll have all the key information at your fingertips.

Set up a system for tracking changes in local laws. This could be as simple as setting up Google Alerts for keywords like "[Your City] food truck laws" or regularly checking local government websites. Laws can change quickly, and you want to stay ahead of any new regulations that might affect your business.

REQUIRED PERMITS AND LICENSES

Tax Registration and Business License

Before you sell your first cup of coffee, you'll need to register your business for tax purposes. This usually involves getting an Employer Identification Number (EIN) from the IRS. You can do this online for free. Your EIN is like a social security number for your business and you'll need it for various legal and financial matters.

To get an EIN, you'll need to provide information about your business structure (sole proprietorship, LLC, etc.) and the person applying (that's you!). The process is straightforward and you'll get your EIN immediately after completing the application.

Once you have your EIN, you'll need a general business license from your city or county. This shows that your business is legally recognized and allowed to operate in your area. The process for obtaining this license varies by location, but generally involves filling out an application form and paying a fee. The fee can range from $50 to several hundred dollars, depending on your location and the type of business.

You'll need to provide proof of your business structure (sole proprietorship, LLC, etc.) when applying for your business license. If you're operating as an LLC or corporation, you'll need to show your registration documents from your state.

The business license application will also ask about your business location. Since you're operating a mobile business, you might need to list where you plan to park your truck regularly or where you'll store it when not in operation.

Some cities require food truck owners to renew their business licenses annually, so make sure you know the renewal process and deadlines. Mark these dates in your calendar and set reminders so you don't forget.

Local Permits

A health permit is crucial for any food business. You'll need to pass an inspection of your truck and your food handling practices. The health inspector will look at your water system (both fresh and waste water), your refrigeration and hot-holding equipment, your food preparation and storage areas, and your cleaning and sanitizing procedures.

Before the inspection, make sure everything in your truck is spotlessly clean. Check that your refrigerator and hot-holding equipment are at the correct temperatures. Have a system in place for storing different types of food to prevent cross-contamination.

You'll likely need to show proof that you've completed a food safety course. This course will teach you about proper food handling, how to prevent foodborne illnesses, and how to keep your equipment clean and sanitized. Some areas require all employees to have food handler's cards as well, so check if this applies to you.

Many cities require a special mobile food vendor permit for food trucks. This might involve an additional inspection focusing on the mobile aspects of your business. The inspector might check the safety of your propane system (if you use one), the stability of your equipment while the truck is moving, and your waste disposal procedures.

Make sure all your equipment is securely fastened and won't move around when the truck is in motion. Have a plan for safely storing hot liquids like coffee when you're driving. The inspector will want to see that you've thought through all aspects of food safety in a mobile environment.

If you're using propane or other flammable materials, you might need a fire safety permit. The fire department will check your fire suppression system, the proper storage and handling of propane tanks, and the presence and condition of fire extinguishers. Make sure you have the right type and number of fire extinguishers and that they're easily accessible.

Parking permits are another consideration. Some areas require special permits to park a food truck, especially in busy downtown areas. These might be daily permits you need to purchase each time you park, monthly or annual permits for regular locations, or special event permits for festivals or other gatherings.

Research the parking rules in the areas where you want to operate. Some cities have designated food truck zones, while others allow food trucks to park in regular parking spaces as long as they follow parking meter rules.

DBA Registration

DBA stands for "Doing Business As." If you're operating under a name different from your legal business name, you'll need to register this DBA name. For example, if your legal business name is "John Smith LLC" but your coffee truck is called "Java on Wheels," you'd need to register "Java on Wheels" as a DBA.

The process for registering a DBA varies by state and sometimes by county. Generally, you'll need to check if your desired name is available, file a DBA registration form with your local government, and pay a registration fee. In some areas, you might also need to publish a notice in a local newspaper announcing your DBA.

Registering your DBA protects your business name within your area and allows you to open bank accounts and accept payments under your business name. It's an important step in establishing your brand identity.

Employer Requirements

If you plan to hire employees, you'll need to comply with employment laws. This includes obtaining workers' compensation insurance, which covers medical expenses and lost wages if an employee is injured on the job.

Requirements vary by state, but most require this even if you only have one part-time employee.

You'll also need to register for unemployment insurance and pay unemployment taxes to your state. The rate varies based on your payroll and claims history.

Setting up payroll tax withholding is another crucial step. You'll need to withhold federal income tax, Social Security, and Medicare taxes from your employees' paychecks and submit these to the IRS. There are payroll services that can handle this for you if you're not comfortable doing it yourself.

You must also verify employee eligibility to work in the U.S. by completing Form I-9 for each employee. This form verifies their identity and work authorization.

Other employer requirements might include registering with your state's new hire reporting program, setting up a system for tracking employee hours and wages, and familiarizing yourself with labor laws regarding breaks, overtime, and minimum wage.

Required Posters

Most businesses are required to display certain posters informing employees of their rights. Even if you're the only person working in your coffee truck, it's a good idea to have these posted. They usually cover topics like minimum wage, workplace safety (OSHA regulations), anti-discrimination laws, and employee rights under the Fair Labor Standards Act.

You can usually get these posters for free from government websites or for a small fee from companies that provide updated sets of all required posters. Make sure you get the correct posters for your state, as requirements can vary.

In a small space like a food truck, you might not have room to display all these posters prominently. In that case, you could create a binder with all the required information and make sure your employees know where to find it.

Miscellaneous Permits

Depending on your location and business model, you might need additional permits. If you play music in your truck, you might need a music license from organizations like ASCAP or BMI. This covers the copyright for the music you play.

Some cities have rules about the size and type of signs you can use on your truck. This might include restrictions on lighted or flashing signs, the percentage of your truck that can be covered in signage, or the content of your signs (some areas prohibit certain types of advertising).

You might need a wastewater disposal permit to legally dispose of your coffee grounds and other waste. Some areas require food trucks to dispose of wastewater only at approved facilities.

If you use a generator to power your truck, some cities require a special permit. This often involves noise level restrictions, so you might need to invest in a quieter generator or find ways to muffle the sound.

INSURANCE NEEDS
Questions to Ask

When shopping for insurance, it's important to ask the right questions to make sure you're getting the coverage you need. Start by asking what types of coverage other coffee truck owners in your area have. This can give you a baseline for what's typical in your market.

Ask about what situations are covered and what's excluded. Insurance policies can have a lot of fine print, so make sure you understand exactly what you're paying for. For example, does your policy cover damage to your equipment if your truck is in an accident? What about if someone gets sick from drinking your coffee?

Find out how much coverage you need. This will depend on factors like the value of your truck and equipment, how many employees you have, and what kind of risks you face in your day-to-day operations.

Ask about ways to lower your premiums. Many insurance companies offer discounts for things like having a clean driving record, installing security systems, or taking safety courses.

Understanding the claims process is crucial. Ask how quickly claims are typically processed and what kind of documentation you'll need to provide if you ever need to make a claim.

It's also a good idea to ask if the insurance company has experience insuring food trucks specifically. They'll be more familiar with the unique risks and requirements of your business.

Finally, ask how quickly they can provide certificates of insurance if you need them for an event. Some events require proof of insurance, and you don't want to miss out on an opportunity because you can't get the paperwork in time.

Typical Coverage

General Liability Insurance is a must-have for any business. It covers accidents that might happen around your truck, like if a customer slips and falls. It typically covers medical expenses for injured parties, legal defense costs if you're sued, and property damage you might cause to others.

Product Liability Insurance protects you if someone gets sick from your coffee or food. It covers medical expenses for affected customers, legal defense costs, and settlements or judgments against your business. This is particularly important for a food business, as even a small mistake in food handling could lead to illness and potential lawsuits.

Commercial Auto Insurance is essential for your coffee truck. Regular car insurance usually doesn't cover commercial use, so you'll need a policy specifically designed for business vehicles. It typically includes collision coverage (for accidents), comprehensive coverage (for theft, vandalism, etc.), and liability coverage for accidents you cause. Make sure your policy covers your truck both when it's parked and when it's in motion.

Property Insurance protects your equipment and inventory in case of theft or damage. This is crucial for a coffee truck, as your equipment is expensive and essential to your business. Make sure your policy covers your coffee equipment, your inventory of coffee beans and other supplies, and any improvements you've made to your truck. Some policies might also cover loss of income if your equipment is damaged and you can't operate.

Business Interruption Insurance can help cover your losses if you can't operate due to unforeseen circumstances, like severe weather or equipment breakdown. It might cover lost income, ongoing expenses like loan payments, and temporary relocation costs if you need to operate from a different location. This can be a lifesaver if you're forced to shut down for an extended period.

Workers' Compensation Insurance is usually required by law if you have employees. It covers medical expenses for work-related injuries or illnesses, a portion of lost wages for injured employees, and legal costs if an employee sues over a work-related injury. Even if you're the only person working in your truck right now, it's good to know about this for when you expand.

You might also want to consider Cyber Liability Insurance, especially if you handle customer data or take online orders. This can protect you if your business falls victim to a cyber attack or data breach.

Additional Insured Certificates

Some events or locations where you park your truck might ask to be listed as "additional insured" on your insurance policy. This protects them in case they're named in a lawsuit involving your business. Your insurance company can provide these certificates, often for a small fee.

You might need an additional insured certificate for special events or festivals. The event organizers want to make sure they're protected if something goes wrong with one of the vendors.

When parking regularly on private property, the property owner might request to be added as an additional insured. This is common if you have a regular spot in a parking lot or on someone's property.

You might also need these certificates when entering into contracts with other businesses or organizations. For example, if you're providing coffee for a corporate event, the company might want to be listed as an additional insured for the duration of the event.

Make sure your insurance company can provide these certificates quickly, as some opportunities might come up with short notice. Some insurance companies can generate these certificates instantly online, while others might take a day or two to process the request.

Keep in mind that being an additional insured is different from being a policy holder. The additional insured entity is covered under your policy for specific situations, but they don't have the full rights and responsibilities of the policy holder.

It's a good idea to keep a file of all the additional insured certificates you've issued. This can help you keep track of your business relationships and make sure you're not forgetting to renew any important certificates.

Navigating the legal requirements for your coffee truck might seem daunting at first. There's a lot to keep track of, from permits and licenses to insurance and employee regulations. But taking the time to understand and comply with these rules will set a strong foundation for your business.

Think of it this way: every permit you obtain, every inspection you pass, and every insurance policy you secure is a step towards making your coffee truck dream a reality. These aren't just hoops to jump through - they're ways to show your customers and your community that you're serious about your business and committed to doing things the right way.

As you work through these legal requirements, don't hesitate to ask for help.

Reach out to local business organizations, connect with other food truck owners, or consult with professionals like lawyers or insurance agents. They can provide valuable insights and help you navigate any tricky situations.

CHAPTER 6
MARKETING STRATEGIES FOR SUCCESS

Marketing your coffee is important. It's how you'll attract customers, build loyalty, and grow your business. Let's dive into some effective marketing strategies that will help your coffee truck stand out in a crowded market.

PREPARATORY WORK
Competitor Analysis

Before you start marketing, you need to know what you're up against. Look at other coffee trucks and shops in your area. What are they doing well? Where are they falling short?

Visit their locations and try their coffee. How's the quality? How do they interact with customers? Pay attention to the little things, like how long it takes to get your order or if the staff remembers regular customers' names.

Check their prices. Are they higher or lower than what you plan to charge? What specials do they offer? Do they have loyalty programs or discounts for frequent customers?

Look at their menu. What drinks are popular? Is there something missing that you could offer? Maybe they don't have any dairy-free options, or perhaps they're missing out on trendy drinks like matcha lattes or cold brew.

Study their branding. How do they present themselves? What's their unique selling point? Do they focus on being eco-friendly, or do they emphasize their gourmet beans?

Follow their social media. What kind of content do they post? How do they engage with followers? Do they respond quickly to comments and messages?

Read customer reviews. What do people love about them? What complaints come up often? This can give you ideas for what to do - and what to avoid - in your own business.

By understanding your competition, you can find ways to make your coffee truck different and better.

SWOT Analysis

A SWOT analysis helps you understand your business's Strengths, Weaknesses, Opportunities, and Threats. Here's how to do one for your coffee truck:

Strengths: What do you do better than anyone else? Maybe you have a secret recipe for cold brew or exceptional latte art skills. Perhaps you're great at customer service or you have a prime location. List everything that gives you an edge.

Weaknesses: Be honest about areas where you might struggle. Is your truck older and less visually appealing? Are you new to the coffee business and still learning? Do you have limited funds for marketing? Identifying your weaknesses helps you know where to improve.

Opportunities: Look for gaps in the market. Is there a busy office park with no good coffee options nearby? Could you offer a type of coffee no one else has? Are there events or festivals you could participate in? Opportunities are potential areas for growth.

Threats: What could hurt your business? This might include new competitors, rising coffee prices, or strict local regulations on food trucks. Knowing your threats helps you prepare for challenges.

Use your SWOT analysis to guide your marketing efforts. Play up your strengths, work on your weaknesses, seize opportunities, and prepare for threats.

Creating a Marketing Overview

Your marketing overview is a big-picture look at how you'll promote your coffee truck. It should include:

Your target audience: Who are your ideal customers? Be specific. "Coffee drinkers" is too broad. Think about age, occupation, interests, and coffee preferences. Are you targeting busy office workers, health-conscious millennials, or coffee connoisseurs?

Your unique selling proposition (USP): What makes your coffee truck special? Maybe it's your organic beans, your quick service, or your fun truck design. Your USP should set you apart from the competition.

Your brand personality: Are you quirky and fun? Sophisticated and artisanal? Your marketing should reflect this personality consistently across all platforms.

Your marketing goals: Do you want to increase sales by 20%? Get 1000 Instagram followers? Set specific, measurable goals. This will help you track your progress and adjust your strategies as needed.

Your budget: How much can you spend on marketing? Be realistic and allocate your resources wisely. Remember, many effective marketing strategies, especially on social media, can be done for free or very low cost.

DEVELOPING YOUR MARKETING PLAN

PR and Media Mentions

Getting mentioned in local media can give your coffee truck a big boost. Here's how to make it happen:

Write a press release announcing your new coffee truck. Send it to local newspapers, food blogs, and TV stations. Make sure your press release answers the who, what, where, when, and why of your business. What makes your coffee truck newsworthy?

Reach out to food critics and invite them to try your coffee. Be prepared for honest feedback. If they love your coffee, it could lead to a great review. If they have criticisms, use them to improve.

Offer to be interviewed about the food truck scene in your city. Position yourself as an expert. Talk about trends in mobile food businesses or the challenges of running a food truck.

Partner with local charities or events. The media loves feel-good stories about businesses giving back to the community. Could you donate coffee to a local fundraiser or participate in a community clean-up event?

Event Participation

Participating in events is a great way to get your name out there and meet potential customers. Consider:

Food truck festivals: These attract people who are specifically interested in mobile food businesses. It's a great way to introduce your coffee to a large audience.

Farmers markets: Health-conscious shoppers often appreciate good coffee. Plus, the relaxed atmosphere of a farmers market gives you a chance to chat with customers and build relationships.

Corporate events: Offer to cater office parties or meetings. This could lead to regular corporate gigs or new daily customers.

Local fairs and concerts: Where there are crowds, there's a need for coffee. These events can expose your brand to a wide variety of people.

When you participate in events, bring plenty of business cards and maybe some small freebies like stickers with your logo. These help people remember you after the event is over.

Branding

Your brand is more than just your logo - it's the entire experience you offer customers. Here's how to develop strong branding:

Create a memorable logo: It should look good on your truck, cups, and social media. Keep it simple enough to be recognizable even when small (like on a coffee cup lid).

Choose a color scheme: Use it consistently across all your marketing materials. This helps create a cohesive brand identity.

Develop a brand voice: How do you want to sound in your marketing? Friendly? Professional? Quirky? This voice should come through in all your communications, from your menu descriptions to your social media posts.

Design eye-catching packaging: Your cups and napkins are walking advertisements. Consider custom-printed cups with your logo and social media handles.

Train your staff on your brand values: Everyone who works for you should understand and embody your brand. This includes how they dress, how they talk to customers, and how they make coffee.

Mobile Apps

In today's digital world, having a mobile app can set you apart. Your app could:

Show your current location: This is especially useful if you change locations frequently.

Allow customers to pre-order drinks: This can speed up service and reduce wait times.

Offer a loyalty program: Digital punch cards are easier to keep track of than paper ones.

Provide nutritional information: Health-conscious customers will appreciate this.

Share updates and promotions: Push notifications can alert customers to daily specials or new menu items.

If developing an app seems daunting, consider using existing platforms like Square or Toast that offer customizable apps for food businesses.

Website Development

Even as a mobile business, you need a solid web presence. Your website should include:

Your menu with prices: Make it easy for customers to see what you offer.

Your usual locations and schedule: If you have regular spots, list them here.

Your story: Why did you start a coffee truck? People love to support businesses they feel connected to.

Contact information: Make it easy for potential customers or event organizers to get in touch.

A blog with coffee tips or news about your truck: This can help with search engine optimization (SEO) and give customers a reason to keep coming back to your site.

Make sure your website is mobile-friendly, as many customers will check it on their phones.

Social Media Strategy

Social media is crucial for food trucks. It's how you'll tell customers where you are and what you're serving each day. Here's how to make the most of it:

Choose the right platforms: Instagram is great for food businesses because it's so visual. Twitter is good for quick updates about your location. Facebook can be useful for event pages and longer posts.

Post consistently: Aim for at least one post per day. This keeps your followers engaged and helps you stay top-of-mind.

Use high-quality photos: Invest in a good camera or learn to take great photos with your phone. Bright, appetizing photos of your coffee and food can really draw people in.

Engage with your followers: Respond to comments and messages promptly. This builds a sense of community around your brand.

Use relevant hashtags: This helps new customers find you. Use a mix of popular tags (#coffee, #foodtruck) and local tags (#yourcityname, #localevents).

Share behind-the-scenes content: People love seeing how their food is made. Show off your coffee-making process or introduce your staff.

Email Newsletters

Email might seem old-school, but it's still an effective marketing tool. Use your newsletter to:

Share your weekly schedule: Let customers know where you'll be each day.

Announce new menu items: Got a new seasonal latte? Tell your subscribers first.

Offer exclusive discounts to subscribers: This gives people an incentive to sign up and stay subscribed.

Tell stories about your business or employees: This helps customers feel more connected to your brand.

Share coffee brewing tips: Position yourself as a coffee expert.

Make it easy for customers to sign up for your newsletter by having a signup sheet at your truck and a form on your website.

Contests and Promotions

Everyone loves a good deal or the chance to win something. Try these ideas:

"Free coffee for a year" contest: This can generate a lot of buzz. Make sure to set clear terms (like one free drink per week).

Loyalty cards: Offer a free drink after 10 purchases. Digital loyalty programs through your app can make this easier to manage.

Happy hour specials: Offer discounts during slow times to boost business.

Seasonal promotions: Create special drinks for holidays or local events.

Online Reviews

Good reviews can significantly boost your business. Encourage happy customers to leave reviews on platforms like Yelp, Google, and Facebook. Here's how:

-Ask satisfied customers to leave a review. Many people are happy to do this if you just remind them.

-Make it easy by providing links to your review pages.

-Respond to all reviews, good and bad. Thank positive reviewers and address concerns raised in negative reviews.

-Use positive reviews in your marketing materials (with permission).

Marketing Tips

Here are some additional tips to make your marketing more effective:

Be consistent: Use the same branding and messaging across all platforms.

Tell your story: People connect with personal stories. Share why you started your coffee truck.

Leverage user-generated content: Encourage customers to post photos of your coffee and share them.

Collaborate with other local businesses: Cross-promote with complementary businesses like bakeries or bookstores.

Track your results: Use analytics tools to see what marketing efforts are most effective.

ENHANCING YOUR MARKETING EFFORTS

Making Marketing Fun

Marketing doesn't have to be all business. Inject some fun into your efforts:

-Create a mascot for your truck. A fun character can make your brand more memorable.

-Make funny videos about life as a coffee truck owner. Share these on social media.

-Host a "name that drink" contest for a new menu item. The winner gets their drink for free for a month.

-Create a photo booth area near your truck for customers to take fun pictures. Provide props -related to coffee or your brand.

Health-Conscious Marketing

Many coffee drinkers are health-conscious. Appeal to this market by:

-Offering and promoting plant-based milk options. Highlight the health benefits of alternatives like almond or oat milk.

-Highlighting the health benefits of coffee. Share interesting facts about antioxidants in coffee or how it can boost metabolism.

-Creating sugar-free drink options. Use natural sweeteners or flavor enhancers.

-Using organic or fair-trade beans and promoting this fact. Many customers care about the sourcing of their food and drinks.

Customization

People love feeling special. Offer customization options like:

-A "create your own latte" menu. Let customers choose their milk, flavors, and toppings.

-The ability to adjust sweetness levels. Some people like their coffee black, others super sweet.

-A range of milk options, including non-dairy choices. Cater to different dietary needs and preferences.

-Seasonal "secret menu" items that customers can request. This creates a sense of being "in the know."

Behind-the-Scenes Content

People are curious about how businesses work. Share behind-the-scenes content like:

-Videos of your coffee roasting process. Show how you select and prepare your beans.

-Photos of your team setting up the truck each morning. This gives customers an appreciation for the work that goes into your business.

-Stories about where you source your beans. If you have relationships with specific farms or roasters, highlight these.

-Time-lapse videos of busy service times. Show how efficiently your team works during rush hour.

Customer Engagement

Engaged customers become loyal customers. Try these engagement strategies:

-Host coffee tasting events. Teach customers about different coffee varieties and brewing methods.

-Offer classes on latte art or home brewing techniques. Position yourself as a coffee expert.

-Create a customer of the month program. Feature loyal customers on your social media or in your truck.

-Ask for customer input on new menu items. This makes customers feel valued and involved in your business.

Seasonal Promotions

Change things up with the seasons:

-Create fall-themed drinks like pumpkin spice lattes. Embrace popular seasonal flavors.

-Offer iced coffee specials in summer. Promote refreshing drinks when it's hot out.

-Promote gift cards during the holiday season. Encourage customers to give the gift of coffee.

-Create special blends for different times of year. This gives customers a reason to keep coming back to try new things.

Partnerships

Teaming up with other businesses can expand your reach:

-Partner with a local bakery to offer pastries. This can enhance your menu without requiring additional prep work.

-Team up with a bookstore for a "coffee and book" promotion. Offer discounts to customers who show a recent book purchase.

-Collaborate with local artists to design limited edition cups. This supports the local art community and creates collectible items.

-Work with nearby gyms to offer post-workout specials. Appeal to health-conscious customers.

Event Calendars

Keep customers informed about where you'll be:

-Create a Google Calendar with your locations and share it on your website. Make it easy for customers to find you.

-Use Facebook Events to promote special appearances. This allows customers to easily share your events with friends.

-Send weekly email updates with your schedule. Remind customers where they can find you each week.

-Post your daily location on Instagram Stories. Use the location tag feature so people can easily get directions.

Delivery Services

Even as a mobile business, you might consider delivery:

-Partner with services like Uber Eats or DoorDash for local deliveries. This can help you reach customers who can't come to your truck.

-Offer office delivery for large orders. This can be a great way to build relationships with local businesses.

-Create a subscription service for weekly bean deliveries. This provides a steady income stream and keeps customers stocked with your coffee.

Text Marketing

Text messages have high open rates. Use them wisely:

-Send location updates to subscribers. Let them know where your truck will be each day.

-Offer flash sales or daily specials via text. Create a sense of urgency with limited-time offers.

-Use texts for order confirmations and pickup reminders. This can streamline your service and reduce wait times.

Press Releases

Keep local media informed about your business:

-Send press releases for major milestones (like your first anniversary). Celebrate your successes publicly.

-Announce new menu items or seasonal specials. This can generate buzz and attract media attention.

-Share stories about community involvement or charitable efforts. Show how your business is making a positive impact.

Remember, effective marketing is about consistently sharing your passion for great coffee with your community. Be authentic, be creative, and always prioritize your customers' experience. With these strategies, your coffee truck will soon become a local favorite!

CHAPTER 7
CHOOSING THE BEST LOCATIONS

Picking the right spot for your coffee truck can make or break your business. A great location brings customers to you, while a poor one might leave you twiddling your thumbs. Let's explore some prime locations and how to choose the best spots for your coffee truck.

PRIME LOCATIONS
Coffee Truck Parks

Coffee truck parks are becoming more common in many cities. These are designated areas where food and drink trucks can set up shop. They're often in busy parts of town and can attract a lot of foot traffic.

The good thing about coffee truck parks is that they're made for businesses like yours. They usually have hookups for electricity and water, which can save you money on generator costs. Plus, they often have seating areas for customers, which can make your coffee truck feel more like a café.

Another benefit of these parks is that they attract people who are looking for food truck experiences. Customers come expecting to find unique, local businesses. This can work in your favor if you offer something special.

However, coffee truck parks can also have downsides. You might face a lot of competition from other food and drink trucks. Also, you'll probably have to pay rent or fees to use the space. Make sure to factor these costs into your budget.

Before setting up in a coffee truck park, visit it at different times of day. See how busy it gets and what kind of customers it attracts. This will help you decide if it's the right fit for your business.

Farmers Markets

Farmers markets can be great spots for coffee trucks. People who shop at farmers markets often appreciate locally-made, high-quality products. If that's what your coffee truck offers, you might find your perfect audience here.

One big advantage of farmers markets is the built-in crowd. People come expecting to buy food and drinks, so they're already in the right mindset to try your coffee. Plus, the relaxed atmosphere of a farmers market gives you a chance to chat with customers and build relationships.

However, farmers markets usually happen only once or twice a week. This means you'll need other locations for the rest of the week. Also, some farmers markets have strict rules about what can be sold. Make sure your products fit their guidelines before applying for a spot.

When considering a farmers market, think about the timing. Early morning markets might be perfect for selling coffee to sleepy shoppers. But if the market happens in the afternoon, you might want to focus more on cold drinks or iced coffee.

Business Districts

Business districts can be gold mines for coffee trucks. Office workers often need their caffeine fix, especially in the morning and during lunch breaks. If you can provide quick, quality coffee, you could become a daily stop for many workers.

The key to success in business districts is consistency. Workers like to know they can count on you being in the same spot at the same time every day. This allows them to build your coffee into their daily routine.

Timing is crucial in business districts. The morning rush (around 7-9 AM) and lunch hour (usually 12-2 PM) will likely be your busiest times. Make sure you're set up and ready to go before these peak hours hit.

One challenge of business districts is that they can be very quiet outside of work hours. You might need to move to a different location in the evenings or on weekends to keep your business going.

Also, be aware of the competition. Business districts often have lots of coffee shops. You'll need to offer something special - whether it's unique flavors, faster service, or lower prices - to stand out.

Gas Stations

Gas stations might not seem like obvious spots for coffee trucks, but they can work well. People stopping for gas are often on the go and might appreciate a good cup of coffee for their journey.

One advantage of gas stations is that they're busy at all hours. This means you could potentially operate early in the morning or late at night, times when other locations might be quiet.

However, gas stations can have some drawbacks. The environment isn't always the most pleasant, with car fumes and noise. Also, people at gas stations are often in a hurry, so you'll need to be able to serve them quickly.

If you're considering a gas station location, look for ones on busy roads or near highway exits. These tend to get more traffic. Also, consider partnering with the gas station owner. They might be happy to have you there if you bring in more customers or if you pay them a small fee.

Bars and Nightlife Areas

Bars and nightlife areas can be great spots for coffee trucks, especially late at night or early in the morning. Party-goers often crave coffee to help them sober up or stay awake for the journey home.

If you set up near bars as they're closing, you could catch a wave of customers looking for a pick-me-up. You might also catch early-morning workers heading to their jobs.

One thing to consider in nightlife areas is safety. Make sure you feel comfortable operating in these areas late at night. You might want to hire an extra person to help you feel more secure.

Also, be prepared for some rowdy customers. Late-night partiers might not be as polite as your daytime office crowd. Make sure you and your staff are ready to handle different types of customers.

Festivals and Events

Festivals and events can be fantastic opportunities for coffee trucks. These gatherings bring together large crowds of people who are out to have a good time and often willing to try new things.

Music festivals, art fairs, sporting events, and community celebrations are all potential gold mines for a coffee truck. People at these events often need a caffeine boost to keep their energy up.

One great thing about festivals is that they often last all day or even multiple days. This means you have the potential for steady business throughout the event. However, be prepared for intense periods of work. Festival crowds can come in waves, and you'll need to be ready to serve a lot of people quickly.

When applying for festivals, start early. Popular events often book their food vendors months in advance. Also, be prepared to pay a fee for your spot. Make sure to factor this into your pricing to ensure you still make a profit.

College Campuses

College campuses can be excellent locations for coffee trucks. Students and staff often need coffee to fuel long study sessions or early morning classes. Plus, college students are often open to trying new and unique coffee drinks.

One advantage of college campuses is the regular schedule. You can count on busy periods between classes and during exam times. However, be aware that business might slow down during holidays and summer breaks.

To succeed on a college campus, you'll need to cater to student tastes and budgets. Consider offering student discounts or creating special drinks named after campus landmarks or events.

Before setting up on a college campus, check with the administration. Many colleges have rules about outside vendors operating on campus. You might need to get special permission or partner with the college's food service provider.

EVALUATING LOCATIONS

Location Assessment

When you're considering a new location for your coffee truck, there are several factors to assess. First, look at the foot traffic. How many people pass by this spot in an hour? More importantly, are they the kind of people who would buy your coffee?

Next, consider the competition. Are there other coffee shops or food trucks nearby? If so, how busy are they? While some competition can be good (it shows there's demand), too much might make it hard for your business to stand out.

Think about parking and accessibility. Is there a safe place for your truck to park? Can customers easily walk up to your window? If you're in a busy area, make sure there's enough space for a line to form without blocking sidewalks or roads.

Consider the time of day when the location is busiest. Does this match up with when you want to operate? Some spots might be great in the morning but dead in the afternoon, or vice versa.

Look at the surrounding businesses. Office buildings could mean a steady stream of workers needing their coffee fix. Shops and restaurants might bring in customers looking for a post-shopping or pre-dinner pick-me-up.

Don't forget about utilities. If you need to plug in your equipment, is there access to electricity? If not, you'll need to factor in the cost of running a generator.

Finally, think about the overall vibe of the area. Does it match your brand? A quirky, artsy coffee truck might do well in a bohemian neighborhood but might feel out of place in a more corporate area.

Popular Events

Popular events can be great opportunities for your coffee truck, but they require careful planning. Start by researching events in your area. Look for things like music festivals, food fairs, sporting events, and holiday celebrations.

When considering an event, think about its size and duration. A small, one-day event might not be worth the effort of moving your truck, while a large, multi-day festival could bring in significant profits.

Consider the audience of the event. A health and wellness fair might be perfect if you offer organic, fair-trade coffee and healthy snacks. A late-night music festival could be great if you specialize in espresso drinks that help people stay awake.

Think about the weather, too. Outdoor events can be great in good weather, but have a plan for rain or extreme heat. You might need to offer more cold drinks on hot days or have a tent to protect customers from rain.

Look into the costs associated with events. Many charge fees for vendors, which can range from a few hundred to several thousand dollars. Make sure you can sell enough coffee to cover these fees and still make a profit.

Also, find out what the event provides. Do they offer electricity hookups? Is there water available? Will they advertise your presence? All of these factors can affect your decision and your preparation.

Finally, consider the competition at the event. How many other coffee vendors will be there? If there are too many, you might struggle to stand out. But if you're the only one, you could have a very successful day.

FESTIVAL APPLICATIONS
Application Process

Applying to be a vendor at festivals can seem complicated, but breaking it down into steps makes it manageable. Here's what you need to know:

Start early. Many popular festivals begin accepting applications months before the event. Set reminders for yourself so you don't miss deadlines.

Read the application carefully. Each festival has its own rules and requirements. Some might want photos of your truck, while others might ask for a sample menu. Give them exactly what they ask for.

Be prepared with your paperwork. Most festivals will want to see your business license, health permits, and proof of insurance. Keep digital copies of these documents so you can easily attach them to online applications.

Highlight what makes you unique. Festivals often get many applications from food vendors. Explain why your coffee truck would be a great addition to their event. Do you use local beans? Offer unusual flavors? Have a particularly eye-catching truck? Make sure to mention it.

Be clear about your power needs. Festivals need to know if you require electricity and how much. If you can operate without external power, make sure to mention this as it can be a big plus.

Provide accurate measurements of your truck. Festivals need to know how much space to allocate for you. Include any additional space you need for signs or seating.

Be honest about your capacity. Don't promise more than you can deliver. If you can serve 100 customers per hour, say that. Don't claim you can serve 200 if you can't consistently hit that number.

Follow up. If you haven't heard back within the timeframe mentioned in the application, it's okay to send a polite inquiry. Sometimes applications get lost in the shuffle.

Tips for Success

Once you've submitted your application, there are a few things you can do to increase your chances of success:

Build relationships. If possible, attend the festival as a customer the year before you apply. Introduce yourself to the organizers and other vendors. Personal connections can sometimes give you an edge.

Offer something special for the festival. Could you create a drink that ties into the festival's theme? Or offer a discount to anyone who shows a festival ticket? This shows you're willing to go the extra mile.

Be flexible. If the organizers ask if you can change your menu or move to a different spot, try to accommodate them if possible. Flexibility can make you a favorite with event planners.

Have a strong social media presence. Many festivals check out vendors' social media accounts. Regular posts showing your products and happy customers can work in your favor.

Be professional in all your communications. Respond promptly to emails or calls from the festival organizers. Even if you don't get accepted this year, leaving a good impression could help you in the future.

Consider offering a revenue share. Some festivals prefer vendors who offer a percentage of their sales rather than a flat fee. If you're confident in your ability to sell, this could work in your favor.

Have a rain plan. If it's an outdoor festival, explain how you'll operate in bad weather. This shows the organizers that you're prepared for all scenarios.

Provide references. If you've participated in other festivals or events, include contact information for the organizers. Positive reviews from other events can greatly increase your chances of being accepted.

Be persistent. If you don't get accepted the first time, ask for feedback. Use this information to improve your application for next year. Many successful vendors had to apply several times before being accepted to their dream festivals.

Remember, choosing the right locations for your coffee truck is an ongoing process. What works well in the summer might not be as good in the winter. A spot that's perfect when you're starting out might become too small as your business grows. Stay flexible and always be on the lookout for new opportunities.

CHAPTER 8
CRAFTING THE PERFECT MENU

Your menu is more than just a list of drinks and prices. It's a powerful tool that can make or break your coffee truck business. A well-crafted menu can boost sales, highlight your best offerings, and create a lasting impression on your customers. Let's dive into the art and science of creating a menu that will make your coffee truck stand out.

MENU BASICS

Theme and Space Considerations

When creating your menu, start by thinking about your coffee truck's theme. Are you going for a rustic, artisanal vibe? Or maybe a sleek, modern feel? Your menu should match the overall style of your truck. This creates a cohesive experience for your customers and reinforces your brand.

For example, if your coffee truck has a vintage theme, you might design your menu to look like an old newspaper or use a typewriter-style font. If you're going for a more modern look, a clean, minimalist design with lots of white space could work well.

Next, consider the space you have available to display your menu. Coffee trucks often have limited space, so you need to be strategic. You might have a small menu board inside the truck, plus a larger one outside for customers to read while they're in line.

Think about how your menu will be read. Will customers be standing close to it or reading from a distance? This will affect the size of your font and how much information you can include. If space is really tight, you might need to have a simplified menu board with your most popular items, and a more detailed menu available on request or through a QR code.

Don't forget about lighting. If you operate early in the morning or late at night, make sure your menu is well-lit and easy to read in low light conditions. LED menu boards can be a good solution for this.

Pricing Strategies

Pricing your menu items correctly is crucial for your business's success. You need to find the sweet spot between making a profit and keeping your prices competitive. Here's how to approach pricing:

Start by calculating your costs. This includes the cost of ingredients, labor, and overhead (like truck payments, fuel, and permits). For each menu item, add up these costs to get your "cost per item."

Next, decide on your desired profit margin. A common rule of thumb in the food industry is to price items at about 3 times the cost. So if a latte costs you $2 to make (including all costs), you might price it at $6.

However, don't just apply this rule blindly. Look at what your competitors are charging. If everyone else is selling lattes for $4, you might have a hard time selling yours for $6 unless you can clearly justify the higher price (like using premium beans or offering larger sizes).

Consider using psychological pricing. This means setting prices just below a round number, like $3.95 instead of $4.00. Many customers perceive these prices as being significantly lower, even though the difference is minimal.

Think about offering different sizes at different price points. This gives customers options and can increase your overall sales. For example, you might offer a small latte for $3.50, a medium for $4.25, and a large for $5.00.

Don't be afraid to price your signature or premium items higher. If you have a special blend or a complex drink that you're known for, customers are often willing to pay more for it.

Consider bundle pricing. Offering a coffee and pastry combo at a slight discount can encourage customers to buy more and increase your average transaction value.

Remember, your prices aren't set in stone. Be prepared to adjust them based on customer feedback and your actual sales data. If a particular item isn't selling well, you might need to lower the price or improve its perceived value.

Conversely, if you're constantly selling out of something, that might be a sign you can raise the price a bit.

MENU DESIGN

Highlighting Star Items

Every coffee truck has its standout offerings - those drinks or snacks that you're particularly proud of or that customers love. Your menu should draw attention to these star items. Here's how:

Use a larger font or different color for your best sellers. This makes them stand out visually and draws the customer's eye.

Place your star items in the "golden triangle" of your menu. This is the area where people's eyes naturally go first - typically the upper right corner of a menu.

Consider adding a "Chef's Recommendations" or "Customer Favorites" section. This not only highlights your best items but also helps indecisive customers make a choice.

Use descriptive language for these items. Instead of just "Latte," you might say "Our Famous Creamy Vanilla Latte."

If you have seasonal specials or limited-time offers, give them prime real estate on your menu. You can create a special box or use eye-catching graphics to make them pop.

Don't overdo it, though. If everything on your menu is highlighted as special, nothing will stand out. Choose a few (3-5) items to emphasize.

Visual Appeal

A visually appealing menu can make your offerings more enticing and easier to navigate. Here are some tips for creating an attractive menu:

Use high-quality images sparingly. A few well-placed photos of your most photogenic drinks can be very effective. But don't overdo it - too many photos can make your menu look cluttered.

Incorporate your brand colors. This ties your menu into your overall branding and creates a cohesive look.

Use white space effectively. Don't cram every inch of your menu with text or images. Leaving some blank space makes the menu easier to read and can create a more upscale feel.

Consider using icons or small illustrations. These can quickly communicate information (like if a drink is hot or cold, or if it's vegan-friendly) without taking up much space.

Group similar items together. This makes it easier for customers to find what they're looking for. You might have sections for hot drinks, cold drinks, and food items.

Use boxes or lines to separate different sections of your menu. This helps guide the reader's eye and keeps the menu organized.

If you're using a digital menu board, consider incorporating some movement. Subtle animations can draw attention to special offers or new items.

Proofreading

Nothing undermines the professionalism of your menu faster than spelling mistakes or grammatical errors. Here's how to ensure your menu is error-free:

Read through your menu multiple times. It's easy to miss errors when you're familiar with the content, so take breaks between readings.

Read your menu out loud. This can help you catch awkward phrasing or missing words.

Use spell-check, but don't rely on it entirely. It won't catch everything, especially if you're using specialized coffee terms.

Have someone else proofread your menu. A fresh pair of eyes can often spot errors you've overlooked.

Double-check all prices and make sure they're consistent. If you list a latte for $4 in one place and $4.50 in another, it will confuse customers.

Verify that all menu items are listed correctly and consistently. If you call something a "Caramel Macchiato" in one place, don't call it a "Macchiato with Caramel" somewhere else.

Check that all promised ingredients are actually included in the item descriptions. If you say your turkey sandwich comes with avocado, make sure that's true.

Concise Descriptions

When it comes to menu descriptions, less is often more. You want to give customers enough information to make a choice, but not overwhelm them with details. Here's how to write effective, concise descriptions:

Focus on the key components of each item. For a coffee drink, you might mention the type of coffee, any flavorings, and the type of milk used.

Use appetizing adjectives, but don't go overboard. "Rich, dark espresso" sounds more appealing than just "espresso," but "our incredibly rich, intensely dark, supremely robust espresso" is too much.

Highlight any unique or premium ingredients. If you use single-origin beans or organic milk, mention it.

Keep it short. Aim for no more than 1-2 lines per item. Remember, customers often make quick decisions, especially at a coffee truck.

Use familiar language. Unless your target audience is coffee connoisseurs, avoid overly technical terms. Instead of "single-origin Yirgacheffe with notes of bergamot and jasmine," you might say "Ethiopian coffee with floral and citrus flavors."

Mention preparation methods if they're unique or add value. "Cold-brewed for 24 hours" or "hand-pulled espresso" can make an item sound more appealing.

If space allows, include any customization options. For example, "Available with your choice of milk: whole, skim, almond, or oat."

Font and Color Choices

The fonts and colors you use on your menu can significantly impact its readability and appeal. Here are some tips:

Choose a clear, easy-to-read font for the main text of your menu. Sans-serif fonts like Arial or Helvetica are often good choices for menus.

You can use a more decorative font for headers or your coffee truck's name, but make sure it's still readable.

Stick to 2-3 fonts maximum. Using too many different fonts can make your menu look cluttered and unprofessional.

Make sure your font size is large enough to read from a distance. Remember, customers might be reading your menu while standing in line.

Use contrasting colors for your text and background. Dark text on a light background (or vice versa) is usually easiest to read.

Incorporate your brand colors, but don't let them overshadow the menu content. The most important thing is that customers can easily read and understand your offerings.

Be consistent with your color choices. Use the same color for all prices, for example, or use one color for hot drinks and another for cold drinks.

Consider color psychology. Warm colors like red and orange can stimulate appetite, while cool colors like blue and green can create a calm, refreshing feel.

Avoid using red text on a blue background (or vice versa), as this combination can be hard to read and even appear to vibrate.

Feedback and Testing

Before you finalize your menu, it's crucial to get feedback and do some testing. Here's how:

Show your draft menu to friends, family, and potential customers. Ask them what stands out, if anything is confusing, and if the menu makes them want to buy something.

Do a "five-second test." Show someone the menu for just five seconds, then ask them what they remember. This can help you see if your key items are standing out.

If possible, do a trial run with a small group. Have them order from your menu and time how long it takes. If people are taking too long to decide, you might need to simplify your menu.

Ask your staff for input. They'll be using the menu every day, so their perspective is valuable.

Consider doing an A/B test if you're using a digital menu board. Create two slightly different versions and see which one leads to more sales.

Be open to constructive criticism. If multiple people are confused by something on your menu, it's probably worth changing.

Using Numbers

Numbers can be a powerful tool on your menu when used correctly. Here's how to make the most of them:

Use numerals instead of spelling out numbers. "5" takes up less space and is quicker to read than "five."

If you're listing calories or other nutritional information, be consistent in where you place this information for each item.

Consider using numbers to indicate spice levels or caffeine content. For example, you might use coffee bean icons, with more beans indicating a stronger coffee.

If you have combo meals or bundles, clearly show the savings. For example: "Coffee + Muffin: $6 (Save $2)"

Be strategic about the number of items in each category. Odd numbers of choices (like 3 or 5) are often more appealing to customers than even numbers.

If you use numbered menu items, make sure the numbers are clearly visible and in a logical order.

Clear labeling

Clear labeling can help customers quickly find what they're looking for and make informed choices. Here are some tips:

Use icons to indicate common dietary preferences or restrictions. For example, you might use a leaf icon for vegan items or a wheat icon for gluten-free options.

Clearly mark which drinks are served hot and which are cold. You could use different colors or simple hot/cold icons.

If you offer customization options (like different milks or flavored syrups), make sure this is clearly indicated.

If you have a signature or house specialty drink, label it as such. This can help guide undecided customers.

Consider using a spice scale for items that can be customized for heat level.

If you offer seasonal items, make sure they're clearly marked as limited-time offerings.

Be clear about sizes. If you offer small, medium, and large options, make sure this is evident for each item where it applies.

MENU ENHANCEMENT TRICKS

Avoiding Dollar Signs

Believe it or not, the simple act of removing dollar signs from your menu can lead to increased sales. Here's why and how to do it:

Studies have shown that menus without dollar signs lead to higher spending. The theory is that the dollar sign reminds people they're spending money, making them more price-conscious.

Instead of "$5.00", simply use "5.00" or even just "5". This subtle change can make prices seem less intimidating.

Be consistent. If you remove dollar signs, do it for all prices on your menu.

If you're worried about confusion, you can include a small note at the bottom of the menu stating "All prices in USD" or similar.

This technique works best when combined with other smart pricing strategies, like those we'll discuss next.

Pricing Strategies

Beyond just setting the right prices, there are several strategies you can use to encourage higher spending:

Use charm pricing. This means pricing items just below a round number, like $3.95 instead of $4.00. Many customers perceive these prices as being significantly lower.

Price in ascending order within categories. Start with your least expensive item and move up to the most expensive. This makes the higher prices seem more reasonable in comparison.

Consider using prestige pricing for your premium items. This means setting the price noticeably higher than other items. This can actually increase sales of these items as customers perceive them as being of higher quality.

Use anchor pricing. Place a very expensive item at the top of the menu. Other items will seem more reasonably priced in comparison, even if they're still relatively expensive.

Offer bundle deals. A "coffee and pastry" combo priced slightly lower than buying each item separately can increase overall sales.

Use relative pricing to your advantage. If you offer different sizes, make the price jump between small and medium larger than between medium and large. This can encourage customers to "upgrade" to the large size.

Layout Tips

The way you arrange items on your menu can significantly impact what customers choose. Here are some layout tips:

Place your most profitable items in the "golden triangle." This is the area where people's eyes go first - typically the upper right corner of a menu.

Use boxes or other visual cues to highlight items you want to sell more of. A simple box around an item or category can increase its sales by up to 30%.

Group similar items together. This makes it easier for customers to find what they're looking for.

If you have a lot of options, consider using columns. This can make your menu easier to scan quickly.

Use white space effectively. Don't cram every inch of your menu with text or images. Some blank space can make your menu look more upscale and easier to read.

If you use a two-page menu, remember that the back page often gets less attention. Put items you really want to sell on the first page.

Consider using a separate insert for daily specials or seasonal items. This draws attention to these items and allows you to easily update your offerings.

Highlighting Premium Items

Your premium items are often your most profitable, so it's worth drawing extra attention to them. Here's how:

Use a different color or font for your premium items to make them stand out.

Place these items at the beginning or end of each section. These positions typically get more attention than the middle of a list.

Consider adding a special section for "Premium" or "Signature" items.

Use more detailed descriptions for these items. Highlight what makes them special, whether it's premium ingredients or a unique preparation method.

If appropriate, include the origin of special ingredients. "Made with single-origin Colombian beans" can justify a higher price and appeal to coffee enthusiasts.

Consider using a chef's or barista's recommendation for these items. People often trust expert opinions.

If you use photos on your menu, make sure to include images of your premium items. High-quality, appetizing photos can significantly boost sales.

Using Photos Effectively

While you don't want to overdo it with photos, a few well-placed images can significantly boost sales. Here's how to use photos effectively:

Use high-quality, professional photos. Poor quality images can make your food and drinks look unappetizing.

Only include photos of your best-looking and best-selling items. These should be items you're confident will look as good in person as they do in the photo.

Consider using photos to show size differences between small, medium, and large drinks.

If you use photos, make sure they accurately represent what the customer will receive. Misleading photos can lead to disappointed customers.

Use photos sparingly. Too many can make your menu look cluttered and less upscale.

If you're using a digital menu board, you might rotate through photos of different menu items. This can draw attention to various offerings throughout the day.

Remember that photos take up space. If you're tight on menu real estate, it might be better to use that space for more menu items or descriptions.

Consistent Branding

Your menu should be an extension of your overall brand. Here's how to ensure your menu aligns with your brand identity:

Use your brand colors in your menu design. This ties your menu into your overall visual identity.

Include your logo on the menu, but don't let it overshadow the actual menu items.

Use language that matches your brand voice. If your brand is fun and quirky, your menu descriptions should reflect that. If you're going for a more sophisticated vibe, use more refined language.

Make sure any fonts you use on your menu match or complement the fonts used in your other branding materials.

If you have a tagline or slogan, consider incorporating it into your menu design.

Use consistent terminology across all your materials. If you call it a "latte" on your menu, don't call it a "cafe latte" on your website or social media.

If you have any signature items that are closely tied to your brand identity, make sure they're prominently featured on your menu.

Consider adding a brief story about your coffee truck or your coffee sourcing philosophy if it aligns with your brand values. This can help reinforce your brand identity and connect with customers.

Engaging Descriptions

The way you describe your menu items can make a big difference in how appealing they sound to customers. Here are some tips for writing engaging descriptions:

Use sensory words that appeal to taste, smell, and texture. Instead of just "chocolate muffin," try "rich, moist chocolate muffin with gooey chocolate chips."

Highlight unique or high-quality ingredients. If you use single-origin beans or organic milk, make sure to mention it.

Include preparation methods if they add value. "Cold-brewed for 24 hours" or "hand-pulled espresso" can make an item sound more appealing.

Use evocative language, but keep it genuine. "Life-changing espresso" might be a bit much, but "bold, eye-opening espresso" could work well.

Consider adding a brief story or origin for special items. For example, "Inspired by traditional Vietnamese coffee, our Saigon Surprise combines strong espresso with sweetened condensed milk."

Use positive words that create a good feeling. "Comforting," "refreshing," "energizing," or "indulgent" can all work well for different types of drinks.

Be specific about flavors. Instead of just saying "flavored latte," specify "vanilla bean latte" or "caramel swirl latte."

Mention the benefits of certain ingredients. For example, "Matcha latte - packed with antioxidants and smooth, earthy flavor."

Keep descriptions concise. Aim for no more than 1-2 lines per item. You want to give enough information to entice the customer without overwhelming them.

Use active language. "We infuse our cold brew with nitrogen for a creamy texture" sounds more engaging than "Our cold brew is nitrogen-infused."

If you offer customization options, mention them briefly. "Available with your choice of milk" lets customers know they have options without cluttering your main description.

Consider using quotation marks for the names of signature drinks. This can make them stand out and feel more special.

Avoid clichés and overused phrases. Everyone claims to have the "best coffee in town," so try to find more unique ways to describe what makes your offerings special.

If you have vegan, gluten-free, or other dietary-specific options, make sure to highlight these clearly. Many customers specifically look for these options.

Use comparisons to familiar flavors or experiences when introducing unique items. For example, "Our turmeric latte offers a warm, spicy flavor similar to chai."

Don't be afraid to use humor if it fits your brand voice. A funny name or description can make a menu item more memorable.

Remember, your menu is often the first point of interaction between your customers and your offerings. It's your chance to sell your drinks and food before customers even place an order. By crafting engaging descriptions, you're not just listing what you sell - you're telling the story of your coffee truck and creating anticipation for the experience your customers are about to have.

When writing your descriptions, try to put yourself in your customers' shoes. What would make you want to try a particular drink? What information would you find helpful? What would make you choose one item over another? Use these insights to guide your writing.

It's also important to keep your descriptions up-to-date. If you change a recipe or switch suppliers, make sure your menu reflects this. Seasonal changes are also a great opportunity to refresh your descriptions and highlight new flavors or ingredients.

Remember that your menu is a living document. Don't be afraid to make changes based on customer feedback or sales data. If customers frequently ask questions about a particular item, consider adding that information to the menu description. If an item isn't selling well, try rewriting its description to make it more appealing.

Lastly, make sure your staff is familiar with all the menu descriptions. They should be able to elaborate on any item if a customer asks for more information. This consistency between your written menu and your staff's knowledge will reinforce the professionalism of your coffee truck and enhance the overall customer experience.

CHAPTER 9
ENSURING COFFEE QUALITY AND SAFETY

Running a successful coffee truck is about consistently delivering high-quality coffee while maintaining strict safety standards. This chapter will guide you through the essential practices to ensure your coffee is top-notch and your operations are safe and compliant.

COFFEE QUALITY CONTROL

Sourcing Quality Beans

The journey to a great cup of coffee starts with the beans. Choosing high-quality coffee beans is crucial for the success of your coffee truck. Here's how to source the best beans:

Research coffee origins: Different regions produce beans with unique flavors. Central American coffees often have a bright, clean taste, while African coffees can be more fruity and complex. Indonesian coffees tend to be earthy and full-bodied. Understanding these differences will help you choose beans that match your desired flavor profile.

Work with reputable suppliers: Look for coffee roasters or importers with a good reputation. They should be able to provide detailed information about the beans' origin, processing method, and roast date.

Consider sustainability: Many customers appreciate ethically sourced coffee. Look for beans that are Fair Trade certified, Rainforest Alliance certified, or direct trade. These certifications ensure that farmers are paid fairly and environmental standards are met.

Sample before you buy: Most suppliers will provide samples. Try different beans to find the ones that best suit your taste and your customers' preferences.

Check for freshness: Freshly roasted beans make the best coffee. Look for beans with a recent roast date and avoid those that have been sitting on shelves for months.

Consider your menu: If you plan to offer espresso-based drinks, you'll want beans that work well under pressure. For cold brew, you might prefer a different bean altogether.

Don't be afraid to blend: Many coffee shops create their own unique blends by combining beans from different origins. This can help you create a signature taste that sets your coffee truck apart.

Roasting Techniques

The roasting process greatly affects the flavor of your coffee. While you might not be roasting your own beans (at least not at first), understanding roasting techniques can help you choose the right beans and communicate better with your suppliers.

Light roasts: These beans are light brown and have no oil on the surface. They retain more of the bean's original flavor and have higher acidity. Light roasts are great for highlighting the unique characteristics of single-origin coffees.

Medium roasts: These beans are medium brown and also lack oil on the surface. They have a more balanced flavor, aroma, and acidity. Medium roasts are versatile and work well for most brewing methods.

Dark roasts: These beans are dark brown and have an oily surface. They have a stronger, sometimes bitter flavor with less acidity. Dark roasts are often used for espresso blends.

If you're working with a local roaster, discuss your preferences and the types of drinks you'll be serving. They can help you choose the right roast level for your needs.

Consider offering a range of roasts to cater to different tastes. Some customers prefer the bright, acidic notes of a light roast, while others enjoy the bold, intense flavors of a dark roast.

Brewing Methods

The way you brew your coffee is just as important as the beans you use. Different brewing methods can bring out different flavors in the same coffee.

Here are some popular brewing methods to consider for your coffee truck:

Espresso: This is the foundation for many popular coffee drinks like lattes, cappuccinos, and Americanos. Espresso machines force hot water through finely-ground coffee under high pressure, creating a concentrated shot of coffee with a layer of crema on top.

Drip coffee: This is a common method for brewing larger quantities of coffee. Hot water drips over ground coffee in a filter, collecting in a pot below. It's simple, efficient, and familiar to most customers.

Pour-over: This method involves pouring hot water over ground coffee in a filter. It allows for more control over the brewing process and can produce a clean, flavorful cup of coffee.

Cold brew: Coffee grounds are steeped in cold water for 12-24 hours, producing a smooth, less acidic coffee that's perfect for iced drinks.

French press: Ground coffee is steeped in hot water, then pressed to separate the grounds from the liquid. This method produces a full-bodied coffee with more oils and sediment.

Each method has its pros and cons in terms of flavor, preparation time, and equipment needed. Choose methods that fit your truck's space constraints and your target market's preferences.

Consistency in Taste

Delivering a consistent taste is key to building customer loyalty. Here's how to maintain consistency:

Use precise measurements: Invest in good scales to measure your coffee and water accurately. Consistency in measurements leads to consistency in taste.

Control water temperature: Different brewing methods require different water temperatures. Use thermometers to ensure you're using the right temperature every time.

Train your staff thoroughly: Make sure all your employees know how to prepare each drink correctly. Create standard recipes and procedures for each item on your menu.

Clean your equipment regularly: Residue from old coffee can affect the taste of new brews. Clean your equipment daily and descale regularly.

Monitor your water quality: The quality of your water can greatly affect the taste of your coffee. Consider using filtered water if your local tap water has a strong taste or odor.

Rotate your stock: Use the first in, first out (FIFO) method to ensure you're always using the freshest beans.

Taste test regularly: Make it a habit to taste your coffee throughout the day. This will help you catch any issues early.

SAFETY PRACTICES

Passing Inspections

Health inspections are a crucial part of running a food business. Here's how to prepare:

Know the rules: Familiarize yourself with local health codes and food safety regulations. These can vary by location, so make sure you're following the right guidelines.

Keep detailed records: Document your cleaning schedules, food storage temperatures, and staff training. Inspectors love to see good record-keeping.

Conduct self-inspections: Regularly check your truck as if you were a health inspector. This helps you catch and fix issues before an official inspection.

Be transparent: If an inspector does find an issue, be honest and show willingness to correct it immediately.

Staff Training

Your staff plays a crucial role in maintaining food safety. Here's how to ensure they're well-trained:

Provide formal food safety training: Consider having your staff complete a food handler's course. Many areas require this certification.

Create clear protocols: Develop step-by-step procedures for tasks like handwashing, cleaning equipment, and handling food. Make these easily accessible to all staff.

Lead by example: Always follow proper food safety practices yourself. Your staff will follow your lead.

Regularly review safety procedures: Don't just train once and forget. Regularly discuss food safety in team meetings and provide refresher training.

Proper Washing and Cleaning

Cleanliness is crucial in a food business. Here's how to maintain high standards:

Handwashing: Install a proper handwashing station in your truck. Staff should wash hands frequently, especially after handling money, touching their face, or using the restroom.

Equipment cleaning: Clean all equipment daily. This includes coffee makers, grinders, milk frothers, and any food preparation surfaces.

Sanitizing: After cleaning, sanitize all food-contact surfaces. Use a sanitizer approved for food service and follow the manufacturer's instructions for concentration and contact time.

Dish washing: If you use reusable dishes or utensils, ensure you have a proper three-compartment sink for washing, rinsing, and sanitizing.

Produce Handling

If you serve food along with your coffee, proper produce handling is essential:

- Wash all produce thoroughly before use, even if you plan to peel it.
- Store produce separately from other foods, especially raw meats.
- Cut produce on clean cutting boards with clean, sanitized knives.
- Refrigerate cut produce promptly if not using immediately.

Storage Protocols

Proper storage prevents contamination and ensures food stays fresh:

- Store dry goods in sealed containers off the floor.
- Keep refrigerated items at 41°F (5°C) or below.
- Store raw meats below ready-to-eat foods in the refrigerator to prevent cross-contamination.
- Label all stored items with the date they were opened or prepared.

Sanitization

Regular sanitization kills harmful bacteria:

- Use sanitizers approved for food service. Common options include chlorine bleach solutions or quaternary ammonium compounds.
- Follow the manufacturer's instructions for concentration and contact time.
- Use test strips to ensure your sanitizer solution is at the correct strength.
- Sanitize all food-contact surfaces, including counters, cutting boards, and utensils.

Supply Inspection

Regularly inspect your supplies to ensure quality and safety:

-Check deliveries immediately upon receipt. Reject any items that are damaged, expired, or at incorrect temperatures.

-Inspect produce for signs of spoilage or pest damage.

-Check packaging integrity on all products.

-Verify that refrigerated and frozen items are at the correct temperature upon delivery.

INSPECTION PREPARATION

Handwashing Stations

Proper handwashing is crucial for food safety:

-Install a dedicated handwashing sink in your truck. This should be separate from any sinks used for food preparation or dishwashing.

-Stock the handwashing station with soap, paper towels, and a trash can.

-Post clear hand washing instructions near the sink.

-Ensure the water at the handwashing sink reaches at least 100°F (38°C).

Approved Sources

All your food and supplies must come from approved sources:

-Keep receipts and invoices for all food purchases.

-Only buy from licensed, reputable suppliers.

-If you make any items yourself (like syrups or baked goods), ensure you're following all local regulations for food production.

Temperature Control

Proper temperature control prevents the growth of harmful bacteria:

-Use thermometers to regularly check the temperature of your refrigerators and hot-holding equipment.

-Keep cold foods at 41°F (5°C) or below and hot foods at 135°F (57°C) or above.

-Use a probe thermometer to check the internal temperature of foods.

-Keep logs of temperature checks for your records.

Cross Contamination Prevention

Preventing cross-contamination is key to food safety:

-Use separate cutting boards and utensils for different types of food.

-Store raw meats below ready-to-eat foods in the refrigerator.

-Clean and sanitize all equipment between uses, especially when switching between different types of food.

-Ensure staff wash hands and change gloves when switching tasks.

Labeling Requirements

Proper labeling helps with inventory management and food safety:

-Label all stored food with the date it was opened or prepared.

-If you repackage any foods, ensure the new package includes all required information (ingredients, allergens, etc.).

-Clearly mark any food that's being held for return or discard.

Permit Display

Make sure all required permits and certificates are easily visible:

-Display your food service permit where customers can see it.

-Keep copies of staff food handler certificates on hand.

-If applicable, display your most recent inspection report.

Equipment Maintenance

Well-maintained equipment is crucial for food safety and quality:

-Regularly inspect all equipment for signs of wear or damage.

-Follow manufacturer's instructions for cleaning and maintenance.

-Keep records of all equipment maintenance and repairs.

-Replace equipment that can no longer be properly cleaned and sanitized.

Cleanliness Standards

Maintain high cleanliness standards throughout your truck:

-Develop and follow a regular cleaning schedule for all areas of your truck.

-Pay special attention to high-touch areas like handles, switches, and cash registers.

-Keep floors clean and free of debris to prevent pest issues.

-Regularly clean and sanitize waste disposal areas.

Knowledge and Training

-Ensure all staff have the knowledge they need to maintain food safety:

-Provide regular food safety training to all staff.

-Keep training records for each employee.

-Ensure at least one person with advanced food safety training (like ServSafe certification) is present during all operating hours.

-Encourage staff to ask questions and report any food safety concerns.

By following these guidelines, you'll not only ensure the quality and safety of your coffee and food but also build trust with your customers and stay on the right side of health regulations. Remember, in the food service industry, quality and safety go hand in hand. Prioritizing both will set your coffee truck up for long-term success.

CHAPTER 10
GROWING AND SUSTAINING YOUR BUSINESS

Starting a coffee truck is exciting, but keeping it running and growing over time is where the real challenge lies. This chapter will guide you through the key aspects of sustaining and expanding your coffee truck business, from hiring and training staff to implementing long-term success strategies and exploring growth opportunities.

HIRING AND TRAINING STAFF
Recruitment Strategies

As your coffee truck business grows, you'll need to bring on staff to help you manage the workload. Finding the right people is crucial for your success. Here are some effective recruitment strategies:

Tap into your network: Let friends, family, and regular customers know you're hiring. They might know someone perfect for the job.

Use social media: Post job openings on your business's social media accounts. Your followers already know and like your brand, making them potential candidates.

Partner with local schools: If there's a culinary school or hospitality program nearby, reach out to them. Students or recent graduates could be great fits for your business.

Host a job fair: Set up a small job fair near your usual parking spot. This allows potential candidates to see your truck and get a feel for the work environment.

Be clear about expectations: In your job postings, be upfront about the demands of working in a coffee truck. Mention early mornings, weekend work, and the physical nature of the job.

Look for passion: While experience is valuable, don't overlook candidates who are passionate about coffee but may lack formal experience. Enthusiasm can often make up for a lack of experience.

Consider part-time staff: If you're not ready for full-time employees, start with part-time staff. This can give you flexibility as your business grows.

When interviewing candidates, ask about their customer service experience, ability to work in tight spaces, and how they handle stress. These skills are crucial in a fast-paced coffee truck environment.

Training Programs

Once you've hired staff, thorough training is key to maintaining the quality of your products and service. Here's how to create an effective training program:

Start with coffee basics: Even if your new hires have coffee experience, teach them about your specific beans, roasts, and brewing methods. This ensures everyone is on the same page.

Teach your menu inside and out: Staff should know every item on your menu, including ingredients, preparation methods, and common customizations.

Focus on customer service: Train your staff on how to greet customers, handle complaints, and create a positive experience even during busy times.

Practice makes perfect: Have new hires practice making drinks and taking orders before they work with real customers. This builds confidence and reduces mistakes.

Teach food safety: All staff should understand basic food safety principles, including proper handwashing, temperature control, and cross-contamination prevention.

Equipment training: Make sure all staff know how to properly use, clean, and troubleshoot your coffee equipment.

Role-play scenarios: Practice common situations like dealing with a dissatisfied customer or handling a rush of orders.

Ongoing training: Don't stop at initial training. Regularly update your staff on new menu items, techniques, or policies.

Creating an Employee Manual

An employee manual is a valuable tool for setting expectations and maintaining consistency. Here's what to include:

Company history and values: Share the story of your coffee truck and what you stand for.

Policies and procedures: Cover everything from dress code to cash handling procedures.

Job descriptions: Clearly outline the responsibilities for each position.

Safety protocols: Include food safety guidelines and what to do in case of emergencies.

Customer service standards: Detail your expectations for how staff should interact with customers.

Disciplinary procedures: Explain how you'll handle issues like tardiness or poor performance.

Benefits information: If you offer any benefits, explain them here.

Training requirements: Outline any ongoing training or certifications staff need to maintain.

Make sure your manual is easy to read and understand. Use simple language and include examples where helpful. Review and update your manual regularly to keep it current.

LONG-TERM SUCCESS STRATEGIES

Adaptability

The business world is always changing, and successful coffee truck owners need to be ready to change with it. Here's how to stay adaptable:

Keep an eye on trends: Stay updated on coffee trends, food truck innovations, and changes in customer preferences.

Be willing to experiment: Try new menu items, locations, or business models. Not everything will work, but being open to change keeps your business fresh.

Listen to customer feedback: Your customers can be a great source of ideas for improvement. Pay attention to their suggestions and complaints.

Stay flexible with your schedule: Be ready to adjust your operating hours or locations based on demand.

Embrace technology: From mobile ordering apps to social media marketing, technology can help you streamline operations and reach more customers.

Learn from setbacks: When things don't go as planned, treat it as a learning opportunity rather than a failure.

Capital Reserves

Having money set aside is crucial for weathering tough times and taking advantage of opportunities. Here's how to build and maintain capital reserves:

Set a savings goal: Aim to have enough money saved to cover at least three to six months of operating expenses.

Regularly put money aside: Treat your savings like any other business expense. Set aside a percentage of your profits each month.

Keep reserves separate: Put your capital reserves in a separate account so you're not tempted to use them for day-to-day expenses.

Review and adjust: Regularly review your reserves and adjust your savings plan as your business grows.

Consider a line of credit: While it's not the same as savings, a line of credit can provide a safety net for unexpected expenses.

Use reserves wisely: Your capital reserves are for genuine emergencies or significant growth opportunities, not for covering regular shortfalls.

Grand Opening Tips

Your grand opening sets the tone for your business. Here's how to make it successful:

Build anticipation: Use social media and local advertising to create buzz before you open.

Offer special deals: Consider offering discounts or freebies to attract customers on opening day.

Invite local influencers: Reach out to food bloggers or local celebrities to attend your opening.

Be prepared for crowds: Make sure you have enough staff and supplies to handle a busy day.

Collect feedback: Ask customers for their thoughts on your coffee, service, and overall experience.

Follow up: After the opening, thank customers on social media and encourage them to return.

Leadership by Example

As the owner, your behavior sets the standard for your staff. Here's how to lead effectively:

Work alongside your staff: Don't be afraid to get your hands dirty. Showing you're willing to do any job builds respect.

Maintain a positive attitude: Your mood affects the whole team. Stay upbeat, even during stressful times.

Admit mistakes: If you make a mistake, own up to it. This shows your staff it's okay to be honest about errors.

Continually learn: Show your commitment to improvement by learning new skills and staying updated on industry trends.

Recognize good work: Regularly acknowledge and reward staff who go above and beyond.

Local Sourcing and Service Excellence

Supporting local suppliers and providing top-notch service can set you apart from the competition:

Build relationships with local roasters: They can provide fresh, high-quality beans and might even create custom blends for you.

Source locally when possible: Look for local suppliers for milk, baked goods, or other items you sell.

Train staff in coffee knowledge: Your team should be able to talk knowledgeably about your coffee's origin, roast, and flavor profile.

Personalize service: Encourage staff to remember regular customers' names and orders.

Go the extra mile: Little touches like a free sample or a genuine smile can turn a one-time customer into a regular.

Employee Satisfaction and Trust Building

Happy employees lead to happy customers. Here's how to keep your team satisfied:

Offer competitive pay: Research what other coffee shops and food trucks in your area pay and aim to match or exceed it.

Provide growth opportunities: Offer chances for employees to learn new skills or take on more responsibility.

Create a positive work environment: Foster a culture of respect, teamwork, and open communication.

Recognize and reward good work: This could be through formal programs or simple verbal appreciation.

Be transparent: Share your business goals with your team and keep them updated on how the business is doing.

Ask for and act on feedback: Regularly ask your staff for their ideas on how to improve the business.

Consistency

Customers appreciate knowing what to expect. Here's how to maintain consistency:

Standardize your recipes: Create detailed recipes for each menu item and make sure all staff follow them.

Maintain quality control: Regularly taste-test your products to ensure they meet your standards.

Keep your truck clean and well-maintained: A clean, well-functioning truck is key to consistent service.

Train staff thoroughly: All staff should be trained to the same high standards.

Be reliable: Stick to your posted schedule and locations as much as possible.

Effective Communication

Good communication is crucial for any business. Here's how to keep information flowing:

Hold regular team meetings: Use these to share updates, address issues, and gather feedback.

Use a communication tool: Apps like Slack or WhatsApp can help you stay in touch with your team between shifts.

Be clear and specific: When giving instructions or feedback, be as clear and detailed as possible to avoid misunderstandings.

Listen actively: Pay attention to what your staff and customers are saying.

Often, they'll give you valuable insights into your business.

Keep customers informed: Use social media and signage to let customers know about changes to your schedule, menu, or locations.

Cost Monitoring

Keeping an eye on your costs is crucial for long-term success. Here's how to stay on top of your finances:

Track all expenses: Keep detailed records of everything you spend, from coffee beans to truck maintenance.

Regularly review your costs: Look for areas where you might be overspending or where you could negotiate better deals with suppliers.

Monitor your best-selling items: Know which products are most profitable and which might be costing you money.

Watch for waste: Keep an eye on how much product is being thrown away and look for ways to reduce waste.

Consider using accounting software: Tools like QuickBooks can help you track expenses and revenue more easily.

Adjust prices when necessary: If your costs go up, don't be afraid to raise your prices to maintain your profit margins.

BUSINESS EXPANSION

Scaling Your Operations

As your coffee truck becomes successful, you might consider expanding. Here's how to scale your operations:

Add more trucks: Once you've perfected your operations with one truck, consider adding a second or third to cover more locations.

Expand your menu: Gradually add new items to your menu to attract a wider customer base.

Increase your operating hours: If there's demand, consider extending your hours or operating seven days a week.

Hire more staff: As you grow, you'll need more hands on deck. Start with part-time help and move to full-time staff as needed.

Invest in better equipment: Upgrading your equipment can help you serve more customers more efficiently.

Expand your service offerings: Consider adding catering services or selling packaged coffee beans.

Franchising Opportunities

Franchising can be a way to grow your brand without taking on all the risk yourself. Here's what to consider:

Develop a solid business model: Your business should be easily replicable for franchising to work.

Create detailed operations manuals: Franchisees will need clear instructions on how to run the business.

Build a strong brand: Your brand should be recognizable and appealing to potential franchisees.

Understand legal requirements: Franchising comes with specific legal obligations. Consult with a lawyer experienced in franchise law.

Be prepared to provide support: As a franchisor, you'll need to offer training, marketing support, and ongoing assistance to your franchisees.

Start small: Consider starting with one or two franchises to work out any kinks before expanding further.

Diversifying Your Menu

Expanding your menu can attract new customers and keep regulars coming back. Here's how to do it effectively:

Start with small additions: Add one or two new items at a time to gauge customer interest.

Consider seasonal offerings: Introduce special drinks or snacks tied to different seasons or holidays.

Listen to customer requests: If multiple customers ask for a particular item, consider adding it to your menu.

Balance your menu: Make sure you have options for different dietary needs, including non-dairy and decaf options.

Don't forget about food: If you only serve drinks, consider adding simple food items like pastries or sandwiches.

Test before you commit: Offer new items as specials before adding them permanently to your menu.

Exploring New Markets

Expanding into new markets can help grow your business. Here are some strategies:

Research new locations: Look for areas with high foot traffic and a need for quality coffee.

Participate in events: Festivals, farmers markets, and corporate events can expose your brand to new customers.

Consider a brick-and-mortar location: If your truck is very successful, you might think about opening a permanent café.

Explore partnerships: Team up with local businesses or organizations to reach new customers.

Use social media to reach new audiences: Targeted ads can help you connect with potential customers in new areas.

Offer online ordering: This can help you reach customers who might not be able to visit your truck in person.

Growing and sustaining a coffee truck business requires constant effort, adaptability, and a commitment to quality. By focusing on your staff, your customers, and your operations, you can build a thriving business that stands the test of time. Remember, growth should be strategic and sustainable. It's better to grow slowly and steadily than to expand too quickly and risk overextending yourself.

CONCLUSION

Final Thoughts

Starting and running a coffee truck is a journey filled with challenges, rewards, and countless cups of coffee. As you reach the end of this guide, take a moment to reflect on all you've learned. From choosing the right truck to crafting the perfect menu, from navigating regulations to building a loyal customer base, you now have the knowledge to turn your coffee truck dream into reality.

Remember that success in the coffee truck business doesn't happen overnight. It takes time, patience, and a whole lot of hard work. There will be early mornings, late nights, and times when you question why you ever thought this was a good idea. But then you'll serve that perfect latte to a grateful customer, or see a line of people waiting eagerly for your coffee, and you'll know why you chose this path.

One of the most important things to keep in mind is that your coffee truck is more than just a business - it's a part of your community. You have the opportunity to brighten people's days, to be a familiar face in their routines, and to create a space (albeit a mobile one) where people can come together over a shared love of good coffee.

As you move forward with your coffee truck plans, stay flexible and open to learning. The coffee industry is always evolving, with new trends, techniques, and technologies emerging all the time. Stay curious, keep experimenting, and never stop trying to improve your craft.

Don't forget the importance of self-care as you build your business. Running a coffee truck can be physically and mentally demanding. Make sure to take time for yourself, to rest and recharge. Your business will be better for it, and so will you.

Lastly, remember that every successful coffee shop owner, food truck operator, or entrepreneur started exactly where you are now - with an idea and the courage to pursue it. They faced the same doubts, overcame similar obstacles, and learned many of the same lessons you're about to learn. And now, it's your turn to join their ranks.

Encouragement and Motivation

As you stand on the brink of your coffee truck adventure, it's natural to feel a mix of excitement and nervousness. Starting any business is a big step, and there may be moments when you wonder if you're really cut out for this. In those moments, remember why you started.

Maybe it was your love for coffee that led you here. Or perhaps it was the dream of being your own boss, of creating something uniquely yours. Whatever your reason, hold onto it. Let it be the fuel that drives you forward when the road gets tough.

Know that you have something special to offer. Your coffee truck isn't just another food truck - it's an extension of you, your passion, and your vision. The unique combination of your skills, your taste, and your personality will create an experience that no one else can replicate.

Don't be afraid to start small. Many successful businesses began with humble origins. Your first day might not be perfect, your first week might be slow, but each day is a chance to learn and improve. Celebrate the small victories - your first repeat customer, your first day breaking even, your first glowing review. These are the building blocks of your future success.

Remember that setbacks are not failures - they're opportunities to learn and grow. If a location doesn't work out, if a menu item doesn't sell, if equipment breaks down, don't get discouraged. These experiences are valuable lessons that will make your business stronger in the long run.

Surround yourself with supportive people. Share your dreams with friends and family who believe in you. Connect with other food truck owners or coffee entrepreneurs who understand the unique challenges you're facing. Their encouragement and advice can be invaluable.

Stay connected to your passion for coffee. In the day-to-day hustle of running a business, it's easy to lose sight of what drew you to this in the first place. Take time to savor that perfect espresso, to experiment with new brewing methods, to share your love of coffee with your customers. Let your enthusiasm shine through in everything you do.

Believe in yourself and your ability to make this work. You've done the research, you've put in the preparation, and you have the passion. Now, it's time to take that leap. The world is waiting for your coffee truck, for the unique experience only you can provide.

So go forth with confidence. Embrace the challenges, celebrate the victories, and enjoy every moment of this coffee-fueled adventure. Your journey as a coffee truck owner is just beginning, and the best is yet to come. The road ahead may not always be smooth, but with determination, hard work, and a lot of great coffee, you have everything you need to succeed.

Now, it's time to fire up that espresso machine, open your service window, and share your love of coffee with the world. Your coffee truck adventure starts now. Good luck, and may your coffee always be strong, your lines always be long, and your journey always be rewarding.

www.ingramcontent.com/pod-product-compliance
Lightning Source LLC
Chambersburg PA
CBHW071939210526
45479CB00002B/751